The keys to your personal journey in God are tucked away in a quiet Bible book that many overlook or dismiss. You're about to see yourself in the story that's told in the Song of Solomon. With that book as her template, Jennifer Roberts gathers her courage and transparently shows how the journey of the Shulamite in Song of Solomon has empowered her own. Find yourself in this love story and gain fresh perspective on the issues directing your course in life. Your way will be easier because of Jen's honesty—get ready for candid, personal, vulnerable, and gritty.

Bob Sorge

Author, *Secrets of the Secret Place*

Jennifer Roberts in this allegorical commentary on the Song of Solomon has set forth many invaluable truths into how the human heart grows into wholehearted love and obedience for Jesus Christ. She does this in a captivating way that remains faithful to the text and is steeped in rich scriptural truths. As you read you will discover timeless insight into how the human heart grows in confident love, igniting a deep hunger to passionately abandon all to follow Jesus.

Allen Hood

Director of Excellencies of Christ Ministries

Jennifer Roberts is a voice that needs to be heard. I've known her for a few years but known of her for over a decade. Her life has birthed the words on these pages. The Song of Songs is a book often overlooked and misunderstood, yet it holds deep truths for us as the bride of Christ. This book is a springboard for believers to dive into the depths of first love with Jesus. You will be stirred, provoked and encouraged about how much Jesus loves you. Thank you for writing this book and more importantly modeling it.

Michael Miller

Founder and Director of UPPERROOM

The book of Song of Solomon is a book that has formed and fashioned Jennifer's walk and life with the Lord. This book comes from a deep place of revelation and insight into the journey of growing in love for Jesus amid life's highs and lows. I believe that this book will significantly help you navigate the seasons of life with an understanding of what God is looking for in every season. As well, I love Jennifer and would read anything that she writes! She is an amazing woman who has a deep reservoir of truth coming from the Scriptures and her personal journey with God.

Jennifer's husband,

Dwayne Roberts

THE JOURNEY

THE JOURNEY

Growing in spiritual maturity as seen through the Song of Solomon

JENNIFER ROBERTS
FORWARD BY MIKE BICKLE

1st Edition

Four Corners Media

Published by Four Corners Media
FourCornernsMedia.com

ISBN
978-1-7360077-0-9

This book is dedicated to my husband Dwayne whose tireless belief in me is humbling and provoking at the same time. I love you and I love our nontraditional adventurous life together.

To my children you are a tremendous source of joy and friendship it's an honor to be your mother.

To Mike Bickle for fiercely preaching the bridal paradigm and never backing down from pursuing the transforming love of God.

To Laura Souguellis, thank you so much taking hours of transcribed messages and turning them into a readable format so that my book could become a reality. Your commitment to our family has been such a gift to all of us. And we love you. You are an outstanding woman.

TABLE OF CONTENTS

Forward

When I first met Jennifer Roberts she had recently come off the mission field after being with YWAM for a decade in Europe. Jennifer, her husband Dwayne, and their oldest daughter Sydney moved to Kansas City to attend our ministry school in 1998. They planned to attend the training school for a year and then go back to the mission field. But the Lord divinely changed their trajectory.

In 1999, they became the very first staff members of the International House of Prayer in Kansas City (IHOP-KC). I cannot overstate the importance of Jennifer and Dwayne's influence on the house of prayer. They were both on the leadership team for 14 years and had a significant impact on the movement. I saw the Lord shape and mold them into the incredible leaders they are today. It was a sad day at IHOP-KC when the Roberts family left and moved to

Brazil. But the fruit they had in Brazil was extraordinary. I had the pleasure of visiting them and was amazed at all that the Lord had done in Brazil through their lives and the praying church that they had planted.

In their first years at IHOP-KC, I saw Jennifer grow in her love for Jesus and for the Word. She took an even stronger hold of the book of Song of Solomon and the bridal paradigm of the kingdom of God. She made that book her own and began to teach it to others with passion. I have studied the Song of Solomon for many years and have been deeply impacted by the themes in that book and the way that Jennifer communicates it is outstanding.

The Song of Solomon gives us several amazing insights into how the Lord leads and matures us. It is a story about King Solomon marrying a young Shulamite woman. The message in the Song of Solomon magnifies the beauty of natural married love. But it is also much more, it is also a picture of the relationship between the Lord and the redeemed as His Bride (Eph. 5:32; Rev. 22:17). Although this book is often overlooked I think the lessons that we can learn from it are invaluable. It shows us so much about the affection and commitment that Jesus has for His Bride.

Jennifer has dedicated years of her life to the study of this book and its themes. I love the way that she brings in her humor and stories into the teaching to make it more relatable. She has walked through the seasons in Song of Solomon in her own life and the wisdom and perspective she brings from her own journey are amazing.

Although this book does have some odd and at times confusing language, I cannot overstate enough the importance of this book. With the cultural context in mind and the correct interpretation of the book of Song of Solomon, it can change the way you view yourself and the way you view and interact with God. It shows a beautiful bridegroom King who has a deep affection for His people and is ever committed to them maturing in their love for Him. That the Holy Spirit will establish the first commandment in first place in the body of Christ worldwide—even before the Lord returns at His second coming (Rev. 19:7).

I have watched and admired Jennifer for over 20 years now. Her life of prayer and pursuit of the Lord is undeniable. She has spent countless hours studying the Song of Solomon, and you can see how much this subject has impacted her in this book.

I want to invite you to have a dialogue with the Holy Spirit as you read through and study this book. Ask the Lord to reveal the heart of the Bridegroom King to you. Let this book and the words of Song of Solomon speak to your heart and transform the way that you see yourself and how you see the leadership of the Lord.

Mike Bickle

International House of Prayer in Kansas City (IHOP-KC)

Introduction

I discovered Song of Solomon for the first time at age 17. As I had been born again less than a year, I was thirsty for more of God. This book radically transformed my heart then and continues to do so even today, making it one of my favorite books in the Bible.

Song of Solomon depicts the journey of immature love that grows to maturity. Historically, it is about the real romance between King Solomon and a young Shulamite woman, written sometime around the 10th century BC*. Upon further examination, this book also carries a deep revelation of the relationship between Christ and the Church.

The Bride (Church) must journey through testing and maturing until she is ready for the day Christ marries Her. As in real life, the plot of this story is full of ups and downs. What was once a teenage passion becomes a devoted and mature love – a Bride who remains faithful in the tribulation.

This is a story about each one of us. We begin our walk with Jesus as immature and inconsistent individuals. We love ourselves above all else, not knowing how to overcome our own pride. Despite that, if we submit to this process with God, the outcome will be a mature and glorious Bride at the end of this earthly journey.

Some may consider Song of Solomon as flowery and feminine, but this book is for both men and women. It can speak to a woman's heart about a lot more than a projected romance with Jesus. Its content goes beyond the superficiality of earthly love and reveals the perfect love of the Bridegroom. The feminine language that is used does not mean that men cannot see themselves within the storyline as well. This study is intended for all of us who long for a greater measure of Jesus' love.

I have been teaching this content for over 2 decades – previously in the United States at the International House of Prayer in Kansas City (IHOPKC) – and more recently in Brazil at our church, the Florianópolis House of Prayer (FHOP). Many students have been impacted by this message over the years, so I am thrilled to be finally sharing it in this book.

My own stories will be told in parallel with the Shulamite's journey. Many times, I have seen my own walk with God and the various phases of Christian maturity intertwined with the plot of Song of Solomon. This book is not a commentary, but my own understanding and experiences. My prayer is that we become more aware of Christ's love for us, and that His affection would bring transformation and maturation in every stage of the process through divine grace. The immature love in the beginning days of our journey with the Lord could never compare to the devotion that has been tested and seasoned over the years.

A Spiritual Approach to the Song of Solomon

Song of Solomon is a love story condensed in 8 chapters. Solomon wrote 1,005 songs throughout his life, but this one was called the "Song of Solomon", meaning the most important one.

Solomon poetically narrates his romance with the young Shulamite through the use of metaphors and allegories. In this study, all the historic symbolism will be approached as a representation of our relationship with God.

For example, there is a verse in which Solomon says to his beloved, "Your eyes are like dove's eyes" (Song of Solomon 5:12). I would not find these words flattering. My husband, Dwayne, would never compliment me in such a way. In my opinion, birds' eyes are a bit creepy. However, as I analyzed the context and did a little research, I learned that doves have only one partner their entire life. So, this is referring to loyalty. In other words, Solomon is affirming that the Shulamite is loyal as a dove.

It is a representation of the Bridegroom, Jesus speaking to His Bride, the Church, who has eyes for only One. The Bridegroom is expressing His adoration for the Bride as His words become reality in the way that she sees herself. The more that the Bride hears her Beloved declare her qualities, the more virtuous she becomes.

Therefore, as we study Song of Solomon, we need to take the following into consideration:

1) The literal interpretation of the story, which consists of the romance between King Solomon and the Shulamite; 2) The spiritual interpretation intended to correlate the plot with the mutual love between Christ and the Church.

When studying this second approach, I want to ensure that the theme of Song of Solomon is not isolated from other books in the Bible that consider God's love for us. The application of this spiritual interpretation will never contradict the truths that we find throughout the Bible.

Once I was preaching on Song of Solomon in the United States and a man said to me at the end of the service, "I didn't like your message because I do not believe that Song of Solomon can be interpreted in any other way except literally". I responded, "No problem! Go home and tear through your Bible. Even then, you will not be able to escape the fact that God presents Himself as a Bridegroom on many other occasions".

God wants to reveal His heart as a Bridegroom so much so that He compelled Hosea to marry the prostitute, Gomer and have children with her. Even though his wife still went back to prostitution and was repeatedly unfaithful to him throughout their marriage, Hosea continued to love and pursue her.

The Lord said to him, "Hosea, this is how I feel. This is the unconditional, persistent love that I have for my people." This is just one of many instances in the Bible, where God demonstrates strong feelings for us. He is not being poetic when He says He loves us unconditionally.

"And *as* the bridegroom rejoices over the bride, *so* shall your God rejoice over you."

(Isaiah 62:5)

As crazy as it sounds, God is in love with us. He uses the metaphor of marriage so that we can understand His affection for us, since there is not a relationship more intimate than that of husband and wife.

We have so many titles for ourselves in relation to God. We are children, heirs, kings, priests, etc. Each one of these titles carries an identity along with many assignments. Yet, being His Bride was highlighted to me. As a mother, I love my three children exactly as they came into the world. Although, it is different with a bride. She is chosen. She is exclusive.

Bearing the title, Bride of Christ is the greatest proof of His love for us. We were unworthy of the value He placed on us at the beginning of this "romance". But, as He desires us and exhibits His extravagant affection, our heart is awakened in response to His love. Not because we earned it, but because He first loved us.

Understanding the Characters

To interpret the Song of Solomon as an allegory of the Bride's spiritual life, we give each character a corresponding representation.

"King Solomon" is an illustration of Christ, the Bridegroom-King. Though He holds all the power, His heart is full of tenderness and love for His people. He is captivated by the Shulamite commoner and persists in demonstrating his love for her.

The "Young Shulamite" or "Virgin Shulamite" symbolizes the Bride of Christ, the Beloved. She starts out a young, zealous idealist, but her love is tested and matures as her journey unfolds.

The "Daughters of Jerusalem" represent spiritually immature Christians. They have a genuine desire for the Lord but have yet to understand spiritual things. In the story, they look to the Shulamite to learn how to get closer to the king.

The "watchmen" or "guards" represent the religious leadership or authority figures in the context of spirituality. In the story, there are moments that the guards help as well as hurt the bride.

Now that we understand the approach to this study and are somewhat acquainted with the characters, it is important to read Song of Solomon in the Bible and be familiar with the book before we start breaking it down.

1. A Vision of Life

Let him kiss me with the kisses of his mouth
— For your love *is* better than wine.
The king takes me in his chambers.

Song of Solomon 1:2

The Kisses of the Word

The book of Song of Solomon starts with a request. The young woman suddenly comes into the throne room and exclaims, "Let him kiss me with the kisses of his mouth" (Song of Solomon 1:2). Imagine her asking to have intimacy with the Father, the One who influences the requests of the children. She has a limitless zeal, only wanting to make her request known.

In ancient studies, the rabbis used an expression "kisses of the Torah" to refer to the revelation of the scriptures. Deuteronomy 8:3 talks about the words that proceed from the mouth of the Lord. The kisses that the beloved desires symbolize the longing for revelation of the Word. The Bride is asking for the knowledge of Christ.

This initial picture reminds me of the fire of my first days after getting saved as an adolescent. I grew up in a non-

Christian home, in a small town in rural Washington State. My parents were not believers, they were actually hippies. This meant that clothing was optional.

In the hippie philosophy, the priority was to preserve peace and love, even if that meant a life with no rules. Drugs, nudity, and other forms of freedom were normal in my home. To top it off, I was the youngest of 5 brothers. As you can imagine, my childhood and teenage years were anything but normal.

Then again, when I became a Christian, the gospel was different from anything I had ever seen before. Discovering Jesus was like a portal to a whole new universe. During that time, my thirst for the Word of God was so strong that I would read Galatians multiple times a day. I preached to everyone around me and started prayer groups in my school.

I was so radical that the other students would call me a "nun". My zeal would shock people, just like the Shulamite in the beginning of the story. Both of us simply did not know how to manage our passion. A cry for intimacy with Jesus is the first indication of our passion for Him. So, in short, her initial cry of "kiss me with the kisses of your mouth" could be restated as kiss me with the kisses of your words or give me intimate knowledge of the Word of God.

The Superior Love of Jesus

After expressing her desire for intimacy, the Shulamite made a declaration. In other words, she affirmed that her beloved's love was better than wine. Through this statement, she recognized the superior love of the bridegroom in comparison to other pleasures in this life.

Wine is a symbol of delight and pleasure, especially in the time that the story was written. Drinking good wine was something of great value. Consequently, the bride declared that the love of the groom was more excellent than the finest wine. She comes to discover that being with him is more pleasurable than the other things she had known before.

Prior to knowing Jesus, we satisfied ourselves with the things of this world, but now we have experienced and delighted in something that has exceeded all others – the satisfaction that comes in His presence. If you have ever had a personal and (or) supernatural encounter with Jesus, in which you felt His presence and power, you must admit that it is incomparable.

In fact, we were created to have intimacy with the Lord, filling our inner man and giving us new meaning to our existence. The love of God truly satisfies and produces a joy that surpasses all the other loves of this world. This is one of the bride's first discoveries.

When my daughter Chloe was around 8 years old, she had a dream about this topic. She came to me in the middle of the night and said, "Mommy I had a nightmare". Normally, I would be compassionate and go to my kids' room, tuck them into bed again and pray over them until they fell back to sleep. But on this particular night, I was so tired that I just rebuked the spirit of fear and told her to return to bed. The next evening, Chloe crawled onto to my lap and asked, "Remember the nightmare I had last night?". To be honest, I could not and asked her to retell it. Before Chloe shared it with me, she had already concluded that it was not really a "nightmare", but rather a spiritual dream. In this dream, she was at a shopping center with many closed doors. She went to the first door and opened it, where she found lots of shoes and clothes. She proceeded by closing the door and opening another to a room full of cupcakes. Then, she saw Jesus behind the following door, but continued to the next, where she found lots of Polly Pockets. This was Chloe's favorite toy at the time, so she went into that room and played until the dream was over.

By the time she had finished describing the dream, she was crying and said, "Mommy, I didn't choose to go into the room where Jesus was! I picked Polly Pockets instead of Jesus! Just like in Song of Solomon, where it says that Jesus's love is better, I didn't choose His love."

I looked at her little face and thought, *You are eight years old; how do you know what it says in Song of Solomon?* Before I could say anything, she began to repent, "Jesus forgive me because I chose the Polly Pockets instead of You! I never want to choose anything over You! Jesus, take everything away that keeps me from loving you completely!".

This scene left me impressed. My eight-year-old daughter was already convinced of the superiority of being with Jesus. I am not against toys or other fun things. In her own kid universe, the Lord showed her that spending time with Him is better than her favorite toys. In fact, being with Jesus is a pleasure far greater than anything else. Age does not apply nor how we spend our time.

If we do not believe that God is a superior pleasure that has the ability to truly satisfy, we will find temporary gratification in other things. Often times, we are bored with God simply because we have only scratched the surface of what He can offer. We were made to be satisfied by God, so we must feast on him. When discontent in God, we end up distracted by other things that are merely fleeting.

The love of Jesus is better than human love. It is more gratifying than a successful career, an esteemed reputation, numerous possessions, delicious food or beautiful new clothes. If He has not exceeded everything that we have ever experienced, it is because we have not yet tasted His love.

> **"Being with Jesus is a pleasure far greater than anything else."**

Jesus is not only above and beyond the superficial pleasures of life, as drugs, alcohol, and sex. He even surpasses the best things this world can offer. Life has many beautiful experiences that are actually ordained by God. But even the wonderful moments in life are only a shadow in comparison to what we can experience in Christ. I was meditating on the phrase "your love is better than wine" when suddenly I had a vision. In this vision, the Lord was showing me a photo album of precious memories that I hold dear to my heart. The first snapshot was when I was in elementary school and won an award. My heart was so full of happiness and pride. The next image was when Dwayne and I got engaged. I even remembered the sensation of butterflies in my stomach and the feeling of an answered prayer. The next image was the look on Dwayne's face when I walked down the aisle on our wedding day. I could see his collar saturated with his tears. Then, the image of the doctor placing my first-born, Sydney's cheek next to mine. I remembered how she smelled and the explosion of love I immediately had for her. Afterwards, the Lord spoke to me, "I'm even better than these special moments in your life". He not only outshines all the terrible things in this world, but all the ones that he created for us to enjoy as well.

The Dual Approach to the Search for God

Knowing that her beloved's good reputation had been made public, the young woman pleads, "draw me away!" (Song of Solomon 1:4). Among all the virgins, she wants to be the chosen one, to be alone with Him. This speaks of the necessity of developing our own intimacy with the Lord instead of relying on the relationship that others have with Him.

> "Draw me away! We will run after you. The king has brought me into his chambers. We will be

> glad and rejoice in you. We will remember your love more than wine. Rightly do they love you."
>
> (Song of Solomon 1:4)

In the beginning of our relationship with the Lord, we need to learn to go to Him without mediators. We cannot only depend on the corporate gatherings that we have at our Sunday church services. Real intimacy is direct and personal. Each one of us must cultivate the ability to be alone with God and enjoy His presence.

In the phrase "...we will run after you...", the Shulamite expresses her desire to go with the virgins to look for the bridegroom. It seems contradictory because she initially wants privacy but then, wants to follow the bridegroom with all the virgins. This dual approach to the search for God is present in the Christian life. First, we have a private interaction with the Lord, then shared pursuit in the context of the Church.

It is inherent in our journey with Jesus that we unite with the Body of Christ and seek God corporately. This is called church unity. It is not a self-absorbed romance that ignores and isolates from others, but intended to promote unity. This corporate search is also defined as the work of ministry.

Along this journey, it is necessary to embrace both "take me away" and "come closer", which symbolize personal intimacy, and the "run" that signifies ministry. This dynamic exemplifies the maturing Bride as she walks out the first and second commandments. The first, which is to love the Lord with all our hearts, takes us to fulfill the second, which is to love our neighbors as ourselves.

This is what I call the "vision for the life of the Bride". She wants Him to take her away, but at the same time, go after Him along with others who love Him too. Just like the bride, we all need to have a plan for spiritual growth. "Where do I want to be with God?" and "How do I get there?" are the questions that we should be asking ourselves on this journey.

When there is no clear goal or growth plan, we end up being unproductive and frustrated because "we should have read the Bible" or "prayed more". We all fight our own flesh to achieve spiritual discipline, but when we create an action plan, our goals become more attainable.

Throughout the first chapter in Song of Solomon, the desire of the Bride is made known; she wants intimacy with Jesus.

Experiencing His Chambers

The bride's desire for intimacy starts to be quenched. The bridegroom king calls her into his chambers. She is about to have an intimate encounter with him.

When we go to someone's house for the first time, we do not head straight for the bedroom, because it is a private and intimate place. The young Shulamite is indicating advanced intimacy with the bridegroom when she says, "The king has brought me into his chambers." This progression represents our personal encounters when God talks to us in a profound and personal way. It is wonderful to hear from God as a congregation, but it is incomparable to when we feel drawn into a special place, where He tells us specific and intimate things.

When they say "… we will rejoice and be glad in you; we will remember your love more than the wine; rightly do we love you", the voices of the young Shulamite and the daughters of Jerusalem come together and once again reaffirm the delight that is in the bridegroom.

Note that the beloved's earlier revelation of the bridegroom's love being better than wine is now corporate agreement. Once again, the singular perspective becomes plural. The Bride is learning to walk as the Body of Christ.

It is crucial to understand that the bride is both a personal and corporate reality. Who is the Bride of Christ? Each of us… as individuals AND together as a whole. We cannot isolate ourselves from the Body of Christ and believe that the Church is inferior because WE are the Church as well.

2. The Paradox of Grace

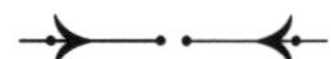

I *am* dark, but lovely,

O daughters of Jerusalem,

Like the tents of Kedar,

Like the curtains of Solomon.

Song of Solomon 1:5

Discovering and Facing our Weaknesses

This entire chapter is dedicated to Song of Solomon 1:5, as this verse is one of its main messages, which is the revelation of God's grace in the midst of our imperfection. At this stage, the young Shulamite comes to an important conclusion when she says, "I am dark, but lovely…". She reveals that her skin is suntanned. In the historical period when this story was written, pale skin was a symbol of beauty. Only the workers were exposed to the sun and tanned while laboring in the fields. For this reason, tan skin was associated with poverty and the working class.

Here, the young Shulamite is becoming aware that she is unworthy of this love. This is the same revelation that we have when we understand that we do not deserve the grace of God.

> "Like the tents of Kedar [they were made of black goat skin], like the curtains of Solomon [they were bright white]."
>
> (Song of Solomon 1:5)

Through the biblical paradox of the grace of God comes the realization of our unworthiness, along with the revelation of undeserved forgiveness. The bride is coming to understand the gift of righteousness.

In the Christian life, this tension is always present. We are conscious of our potential for sin, but freely received the perfect righteousness of Christ. The Word says that justification does not come through works so that no one be glorified, but by faith in Jesus and the work He completed for us.

In our walk with God, it is necessary to understand that our righteousness is not our own, but derives from God. We are not beautiful (virtuous and loved) because we are worthy, but because Christ put Himself in our place and justified us with His blood.

> "For by grace you have been saved through faith, and that not of yourselves; *it is* the gift of God, not of works, lest anyone should boast."
>
> (Ephesians 2:8-9)

> "For He made Him who knew no sin *to be* sin for us, that we might become the righteousness of God in Him."
>
> (2 Corinthians 5:21)

Dealing with Relapses

All of us have thought that struggling with a certain sin was something of the past, but still found ourselves doing it again. Many times, I have uncovered sin and immaturities in myself that I was sure I had already overcome. Yet, the truth is that I will never stop needing God's grace and forgiveness to be able to stand.

Unfortunately, some of us have never recovered from our relapses as we do not grasp God's true grace. Sometimes all we know is a religious image of a severe relentless God. When we fall into sin, the weight of shame is so heavy that instead of running to God, we run away from Him, never to return.

I had a friend in a similar situation. We became close during missionary training with Youth With A Mission (YWAM). She was a determined girl full of opinions, especially concerning issues on abortion.

When she returned from the mission field, she had a hard time readapting to her old church and ended up in a lifestyle of partying. In this context, she became pregnant. Desperate, she found a clinic and made the choice that she used to condemn – an abortion.

> **"Through the biblical paradox of the grace of God comes the realization of our unworthiness, along with the revelation of underserved forgiveness."**

At that time, she came to me and confessed what she had done. We prayed together and I felt hopeful that she would be restored in the Lord. But the feeling of hypocrisy that she suffered was terrible. Time went on and she was never able to forgive herself.

Because of this, she fully embraced a worldly lifestyle, as she became insensitive to sin and gave in to immorality. The last news I had from her was that she got involved with the adult film industry.

This is an incredibly sad story about how self-righteousness hindered someone from receiving the underserved grace of God. Without a healthy revelation of the God who forgives and restores, we will never get over our failures/relapses on our own.

Nevertheless, Jesus died for the worst of hypocrites. There is never a situation that He cannot forgive and completely restore. Our sins and scandals are not shocking to Him, because He already knows everything about us. God is not blind, and he even knows the future. When he died for me, he died for my past, present and future sins. He already proved a definitive sacrifice that would resolve our enmity with Him.

Since the cross, the Lord does not define us by our failures, but by His love for us. The Word of God says that Jesus loved us and died for us when we were still His enemy. In our worst state, He deemed us worth it all.

> "For if when we were enemies we were reconciled to God through the death of His Son, much more, having been reconciled, we shall be saved by His life."
>
> (Romans 5:10)

Letting Jesus Into the Mess

I want to tell a story about how I learned this truth when I was younger. As I mentioned in the previous chapter, I became an on-fire believer and in love with Jesus when I converted as a teenager.

Surprisingly, a few months before I became a believer, my parents had a profound encounter with God and were radically transformed. Not long after, they began to serve in our church and became small group leaders. Finally, we would become a normal family.

During that time, I went to the mission field and was out of the house for 9 months. When I came back, everything was strange. My parents were distant from one another. As much as I thought the problem was with me and that maybe I was out of place when I returned home, the strangeness continued. One night, I had a terrible dream that they were getting a divorce. I woke up from the dream and heard my parents' voices in the living room, so I went to tell them about it. I ran downstairs in search of their comfort but instead, they told me they were in fact getting a divorce, which really confused me. The improbable conversion of my parents was a miracle. How was it possible that they were now separating?

I felt betrayed and angry with God. The divorce broke the perfect storyline that I had envisioned.

Upon returning to my room, I cried out of anger to God, "I don't even know who You are!". The feelings of frustration and disappointment were tremendous. I threw the Bible at the wall and started making plans to backslide; go to parties, sleep around, get drunk. To get back at God. But, in the midst of making these rebellious plans, I felt His presence in my room. Out of the blue, His presence was there. My reaction was "No! Get out of here! I don't want You to see me like this!". I felt ashamed to have Him that close while I was out of control.

I was reading through the Psalms and found a portion of scripture that changed my life and gave language to my struggle. It was Psalm 73:21-26, "When my heart was grieved and my spirit embittered, I was senseless and ignorant; I was a brute beast before you". I read this portion of the passage and thought I am in the Bible! I felt bitter anger, like an animal before the Lord. Then I kept reading, "YET I am always with You; You hold me by my right hand". At this point in the passage, I stopped and WEPT. I couldn't believe that God was with me in the struggle. I was so out of control, disillusioned, and angry that I thought I had chased Him off. But, on the contrary, He was near as He is near to the broken-hearted (Psalm 34:18) and saves those that are crushed in spirit. I had a wrong understanding of God and that moment changed my life forever. This is not an exaggeration. It changed my life. He was with me in my dark hour and I could wrestle with Him, but he wanted me to fight in the palm of His hand. I tasted His loyalty in my moment of crisis and I was finally convinced that I could trust Him. The portion of scripture goes on and says, "You guide me with your counsel, and afterward you will take me into glory. Whom have I in heaven but you? And earth has nothing I desire besides you. My flesh and my heart may fail, but God is the strength of my heart and my portion forever".

"His love does not give up in the darkest moments, in the deepest pit, and the most confusing times of our lives."

With patience and grace, the love of God poured over me even in the moment that I felt like such a sinner. He showed me love when I was at my worst. I cried, repented, and reconciled with God. On that day, I understood that God would never leave me, even though I am unworthy. God's love is unlike the human love that abandons us when it is inconvenient. His love does not give up in the darkest moments, the deepest pits, and the most confusing times of our lives.

Understanding how loved we are leads us to love God even more. Jesus said that "He who is forgiven much, loves much" (Luke 7:47, paraphrased). True obedience does not come from obligation but from knowing His unconditional love.

Even if I had said to Jesus, "Don't love me when I am like this!", He would not have answered my request. I wanted to fix myself before receiving the love of God, but that is not how the gospel works. When we think that we can do a better job of justification than God, we are putting ourselves above grace.

We all know what it is like to have an unexpected visitor show up as we run around trying to clean before they see the mess. Sometimes we do this with the Lord. Even so, He does not want pretense or superficial fixes. Jesus desires to reveal the real situation to us.

Inviting Jesus into our mess means allowing Him to come into the restricted areas of our hearts, like tears of trauma, pain, and shame. It is permitting Him to shine a flood light on what must be confronted in order to be more like Him. Jesus is not asking for only what is pleasing, He wants it all, including the stuff that we do not show anyone. Maybe other people reject us when they see our imperfections, but the Lord will never turn away from a repentant heart. He does not judge us the way men do, because He sees our intentions.

When the Lord talked to the prophet Samuel, He said "man sees the outward appearance, but I see the heart" (1 Samuel 16:7, paraphrased). God perceives beauty in us despite our imperfections. His love has the capacity to see beyond the surface to our hidden value.

A Willing Spirit

While talking about the grace of God, I want to emphasize that it does not give us permission to sin. There are a lot of shallow theologies that explore the concept that grace gives us license to sin. The Word says that grace equips us to renounce sin, refusing worldliness.

> "For the grace of God that offers salvation to all people has appeared. Teaching us that, denying

> ungodliness and worldly lusts, we should live soberly, righteously, and godly lives in the present age."
>
> (Titus 2:11-12)

Those that have a sincere desire to please God will never see grace as an opportunity to sin, but a way to invite holiness. The Lord searches the heart and knows when we genuinely repent. He loves a contrite heart and never rejects it.

There are many examples of this in the Bible. After sleeping with Bathsheba, King David fell into great disgust and repentance. Knowing the forgiving character of God, he humbled himself and fell at the feet of the Lord's mercy. Psalm 51: 3-4, 12 says:

> "For I acknowledge my transgressions, and my sin *is* always before me. Against You, You alone, have I sinned, and done *this* evil in Your sight—That You may be found just when You speak, *and* blameless when You judge. Restore to me the joy of Your salvation, and uphold me *by Your* generous Spirit."

Uphold me by Your generous Spirit is a key request. I believe this is what made David a man after God's own heart. He kept his spirit willing, which meant he was ready to repent and return to the ways of the Lord. He had the fear of the Lord and, even in his weakness, an open heart to be made right with Him again.

Mathew 26:41 says, "The spirit indeed *is* willing, but the flesh *is* weak". In the spirit, we desire the things of God, but the flesh craves the opposite. There is a fight between the flesh and the spirit in our inner man. But this willingness in our hearts, although weak, is what makes us eligible for the grace of God.

Jesus did not save us from hell so that we would take His hand and say, "Thanks but I am going ahead by myself from here on out!". No. He is our constant ally in the battles that we have against our flesh because He overcame sin and left us an example.

When we are dealing with temptations, do not forget that the Lord sees our efforts. If we offer a prayer that says, "Lord give me grace to overcome my weakness", we will reach divine help. We need to remember that as the Bride of Christ, even though we are imperfect, we are beautiful.

3. Spiritual Crisis

The Shulamite: "Do not look upon me, because I *am* dark,

Because the sun has tanned me. Tell me, O you whom I love,

Where you feed *your flock,*

Where you make *it* rest at noon."

The Beloved: "If you do not know, O fairest
among women,
Follow in the footsteps of the flock".

Song of Solomon 1:6-11

Ministerial Exhaustion

The next part of the story talks about the bride's first spiritual crisis. She was carefree and in love, but the first obstacles start to appear. The beloved understands that she did not take care of her own vineyard because she was busy tending her older brothers' vineyards.

> "My mother's sons were angry with me; they made me the keeper of the vineyards, *but* my own vineyard I have not kept."
>
> (Song of Solomon 1:6)

The vineyards represent ministry service/work and the older brothers stand for the most experienced leaders that are apathetic to the passion of new believers. In the story, the brothers get irritated with the bride and make her work for them, to the point of exhaustion.

This detail in the story points to when we are more dedicated to the will of man than to that of the Lord while serving. We begin with the right motivation, but when we least expect it, we are consumed by the demand of human expectations.

In saying, "...For why should I be as one who veils herself..." (Song of Solomon 1:7), the Shulamite is referring to the fact that the peasants only covered their faces when they worked for men that they did not know. This means that, instead of working for her beloved, she ended up working with strangers, losing her sense of nearness to him.

This reminds me of a season when the Lord worked in this area of my life for the first time. I was enthusiastic about becoming a Christian and extremely motivated to give my life for the gospel and leave my mark on humanity. I would daydream about the great things I would do for the Lord, the books that would be written about me and my own greatness. At 19, I went to Amsterdam, Netherlands and my amazing work would begin! I went to a discipleship training school (DTS) with Youth with a Mission (YWAM). After completing the 6-month program, I returned to the states to raise financial support so that I could return to Amsterdam to work full-time. I had just turned 21 when I joined the staff in Amsterdam. I was ready to conquer the world!

My leaders said, "Wow Jennifer! You are really good! You have a leadership gift!". Motivated to be the best and demonstrate efficiency, I kept accepting more and more work, to the point that I was leading 150 people. I had many administrative tasks, even though that is not something I am naturally gifted at.

During that time, I went on a mission trip with a team of 50 people to Russia. It was 6 months after the Berlin Wall had come down. Communism had technically fallen, but not everyone got the memo. Systems were still extremely bureaucratic, and political change would take years to infiltrate normal society. The roads were risky, and we were not allowed to travel after dark or we could be fined. It took 5 days to get to Moscow by bus. During this trip, I had to make breakfast, lunch, and dinner for the team. This involved pulling out the gas burners and cooking along the side of the highway.

We camped just outside of Moscow once we arrived in Russia. There was a make-shift kitchen in the driest area of the camp, which was the bathroom. It rained every day of the trip, my towel never dried, and the inside of my tent was full of mold and slugs. To top it off, I was the main character in a skit that we would perform on the streets.

In this general chaos, something happened. On the leadership team, there was a girl who was jealous of me and believed I was a flirt. Then, there was a guy who liked me, but the feelings were not mutual, which angered him, etc. Suffice it to say, there were some pretty intense interpersonal dynamics that made life difficult. Lies were spread about my character, it was a mess. When I went to buy food one morning, I learned that I had been removed from my responsibilities because I was considered "mentally unstable". I had to give up all my tasks, including my role in the skit, which was consequently given to the girlthought I was a flirt. I felt like a failure and ashamed before the leaders and the other campers.

It was an awful season to say the least. Buying food at the local market amid a country in utter chaos was challenging. The currency at the time was erratic and continually devalued, which meant the grocery store prices were increasing daily and locals could not afford food. I was overwhelmed. One day, while on the bus before the skit, I had a stress and exhaustion attack. The crisis occurred due to sleepless nights, as I was trying to manage the accusations underway. In that moment, I felt humiliated when I had to give my costume to my understudy. As I was considered "mentally unstable", I was removed from all forms of leadership except cooking, which was exceptionally difficult. I began to weep on the floor of the bus. I told the Lord that I wanted to give up on everything – forget about the missionary life and go back to my home in the United States. Everything was lost and my reputation was on the ground. That was when I heard the Lord tell me, "Jennifer, you didn't take care of the garden of your heart".

"A deep repentance came over me and the Holy Spirit showed me what I did not prioritize the right thing."

A deep repentance came over me and the Holy Spirit showed me that I did not prioritize the right thing. I had given everything I had, going beyond my limits because of this necessity to show results and never make mistakes in front of others. I had come to the end of myself to receive human validation.

The Lord not only revealed this sin to me, but other sins that were still in my life since before my conversion. I started to cry and throw myself on the floor of the bus saying, "Forgive me Lord! I am a sinner! Forgive me!". My tears mixed with the dirt on the bus floor formed mud all around me. As the other staff girl was waiting for my costume on the bus, she heard me praying and came closer. In the moment of confessing my sins that I would never want anyone else to hear, she said, "That's right! You really do need to repent for that! Humble yourself!". It was quite the scene. Even though she was the last person I would have wanted there, I no longer cared about the opinions of others, only the Lord.

Seventeen years later, I received a letter from that girl at my house in Kansas City. The Lord spoke to her in a dream about her debt of repentance to me. In that 3-page letter, she earnestly asked for forgiveness. I had already put the incident behind me and never expected an apology, but it was amazing to witness how the justice of the Lord always finds a way.

I tell this story to illustrate two things. The first is that if we are humble and unjustified before people, it will always be worthwhile to stand upright before the Lord. We can be misunderstood and even deemed a liar, but God will be faithful to bring forth the truth in our hearts.

The second is how unhealthy it is to be living in the hurricane of others' expectations. As a new believer, or even an old believer, it is tempting to serve a vision or a leader to exhibit our work, but this should not be the priority. The ministerial success and our recognition from people can become crutches for our personal insecurities.

I have seen many Christians become exhausted because they put their value in what they do, and are unable to say "no". Ministry is hard work, but it should not be exhausting. Finding significance in a role played out in ministry is a constant temptation, but Jesus calls us to more rewarding work that is motivated by intimacy with the Bridegroom. I am telling my story in the context of full-time ministry, but it can happen to someone working any kind of job. It is about the motivation of our heart not what we do.

The Instruction of the Bridegroom

In response to the bride, the bridegroom reappears with encouraging words and instructions for her. This is talking about the constant presence of the Lord in our moments of anguish and doubt. First, he calls her lovely, reminding her of the virtues she possesses. Then, he instructs her to be close to the sheep.

> "If you do not know, O fairest among women, follow in the footsteps of the flock, and feed your little goats, Beside the shepherds' tents."
>
> (Song of Solomon 1:8)

This instruction to avoid isolation from the Body of Christ is important. We are not permitted to wash our hands of fellow believers when they hurt or disappoint us. It is a divine decree that we must congregate (Hebrews 10:25). When the bride felt distant and alone, the Bridegroom told her to stay with the sheep. All of us need a local congregation to keep us free from separation.

The Shulamite had just felt oppressed from her older brothers. This could have kept her in a place of bitterness and offense. Walking in communion with our brothers is the key to breaking isolation. Whenever we seclude ourselves, the enemy has space to plant lies in our thinking and keep us offended by the people that hurt us.

When I returned to the mission field, this biblical passage helped me to see what steps to take next. I felt God tell me to go back to my local church, start a small group with a few girls, and pastor them. This way, I would continue what the

Lord wanted to do in me and through me instead of just staying in my room upset that I was not "conquering the world" for Jesus.

In that phase, being with people who were different from me helped refine my character and balance my zeal. Life in community exposes our selfishness as we learn to forgive while walking with imperfect people. The journey is not exclusively the individual, but the whole Body of Christ. Hence, the bride is beginning to value others.

After instructing her to stay with the herd, the bridegroom compliments the bride. He says that she is like the pharaoh's mares. Even though this does not sound like a desired compliment, the pharaoh's mares were the strongest and most glorious animals of that time. Through this symbolism, Jesus is telling His bride that she is strong and glorious.

> "Your cheeks are lovely with ornaments, your neck with chains *of gold.* We will make you ornaments of gold, with studs of silver."
>
> (Song of Solomon 1:10-11)

The beloved says, "Your cheeks are lovely with ornaments". The face and cheeks in Song of Solomon generally refers to the emotions of the bride. It means that he admires her sincere emotions for him and the fact that she is now learning how to manage them as in her godly character. When he says, "How lovely is your neck" (paraphrased), he is indicating her ability to bow her head, recognizing the bride's submission. Therefore, she has surrendered her will. Often when the children of Israel rebelled, they were called stiff-necked people. Consequently, the neck with chains of gold suggests the purification of her will.

4. The Perfect Leadership of God

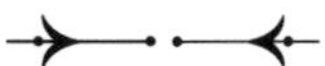

"While the king is at his table,
My spikenard sends forth its fragrance.
I am the rose of Sharon, *and* the lily of the valleys.
Like an apple tree among the trees of the woods,
So is my beloved among the sons.
He brought me to the banqueting house,
And his banner over me was love.
His left hand is under my head, and his right hand embraces me.
Do not stir up nor awaken love until it pleases."

Song of Solomon 1:12, 2:1-7

The King Prepares a Table

In this next scene, the bridegroom is seated at his table with his beloved. She describes the setting as a guest at the banquet that he prepared. The table is not her table, it is the king's. She is enjoying the delicacies that he brought to the table where she is the guest of honor.

> "While the king *is* at his table, my spikenard sends forth its fragrance."
>
> (Song of Solomon 1:12)

Psalm 23:5 says, "You prepare a table for me in the presence of my enemies". This scene refers to the Lord's provision, so that we may walk in victory. The bride did not bring anything to the table, she simply relished what the groom provided for her. This speaks of the benefits of the cross that are free to all that turn to the Beloved.

When the Bride feeds herself from the provision of Christ's table, she does not go hungry – she is nourished. Every time that we feel spiritually malnourished, it is because we are not feeding off the spiritual banquet of the cross. Our hearts "starve" when we do not come to the table of the Lord.

Subsequently, the bride mentions nard and myrrh. Nard is a balm that represents worship. As the Bride meditates on the rewards of the cross, she cannot contain her worship for her beloved and everything He did for her. When we understand the complete work on Calvary, our response is thankfulness and worship to the Lord.

The aroma of the nard spreads throughout the banquet hall. The incense from the nard is like the prayers of the saints that rise to the Lord (Revelation 5:8). The worship of the saints expands across the entire earth when we understand and take joy in the recompenses of the cross. Extravagant worship can impact neighborhoods, cities, and entire nations. The calling of the Church is to triumphantly worship over God's enemies while the He prepares a banquet.

The myrrh represents the suffering of Christ in the crucifixion. Myrrh is a funeral spice used when embalming the body before burial. At the birth of Jesus, myrrh was one of the presents brought by the three kings who adored Him. This is a foreshadowing of the painful death that the Messiah would one day suffer for the salvation of the world.

"Every time we feel spiritually malnourished, it is because we are not feeding off the spiritual banquet of the cross."

When mentioning "A bundle of myrrh *is* my beloved to me, that lies all night between my breasts" (Song of Solomon 1:13), the Bride is expressing her attachment to the cross. What is the first thing that children do when someone tries to take a toy away from them? They hold that toy close to their chest. It is just what we do with things that are precious to us. The beloved is saying that as she continually meditates on the cross, she keeps this memory close to her heart.

In the same way, the Church of Christ should keep the memory of our Savior's sacrifice. Taking the symbolism of communion as a reflection on the memory of how the perfect, sinless God adopted human form. The Word of God that was from the beginning (John 1: 1) came into the world, living the common life, but dying the death of the worst of sinners.

The grave could not hold Him, He overcame death and paid for our sins, giving us the free gift of salvation. This good news will always be the most remembered story in history, especially for us, the Church. In this instance, the Bride is saying, *I will never forget what was conquered on the cross.*

The Exchange of Compliments

The bridegroom affirms her by saying she is lovely twice. This is the image that Jesus is reaffirming His love for us. He always comes back and declares words of affirmation to nourish our hearts. When he says that she has dove's eyes, the groom refers to the loyalty of the bride.

> The Beloved: "Behold, you *are* fair, my love! Behold, you *are* fair! You *have* dove's eyes. The Shulamite: "Behold, you *are* handsome, my beloved! Yes, pleasant! Also, our bed *is* green."
>
> (Song of Solomon 1:15-16)

In addition to what we learned about doves in the introduction, it is important to know that some doves do not have peripheral vision. They can only see what is in front of them. As he compares her to the dove, he is praising her ability to stay focused. She does not have eyes for anyone but him.

Once again, beauty, or 'lovely', is tied to the virtue of being loved. When the bride understood that she was *dark* but *lovely,* she learned that her beauty did not come from her appearance but by the way the bridegroom saw her. This beauty *is in the eyes of the beholder.*

As God possesses infinite beauty, goodness, love, mercy, patience, long-suffering, justice, truth, majesty etc., He gave His own beauty to His creation, which is us. As such, my identity is found in Him, not in myself. All the beauty that we possess came from Him, making it incorruptible.

In a few decades, I will have many wrinkles and faded physical beauty. But, if I cultivate the attributes of God in my character and heart, I will be more beautiful than I was in my youth. It is a timeless beauty that cannot be stolen, as in the following passage:

> "Do not let your adornment be *merely* outward… rather *let it be* the hidden person of the heart, with the incorruptible *beauty* of a gentle and quiet spirit…"
>
> (1 Peter 3:3-4)

Then, the bride responds right away saying, "Oh my beloved, how lovely you are" (paraphrased). The New International Version (NIV) says, "How handsome you are". She is realizing more and more that her beloved's attributes are wooing her. In the same way, the more we know the character of God, the more pleasurable it is to be with Him. It is not a relationship based on obligation, but love.

Many times, I have tried to force myself to read the Bible and pray. Yes, it is necessary to put our uncooperative flesh in its place at times, but communion with the Lord should never be motivated by duty. When we understand the pleasure of being with God, spending time with Him becomes voluntary.

Another highlight from this passage is the way they are exchanging compliments. The bride is returning his affection. The more loved we feel, the more confident we are to tell others how we feel. In the same way, when we feel loved by God, we learn to trust and love Him back.

Consequently, our love for God will result in a life of righteousness. Jesus said, "He who loves me will keep my commandments" (John 14:21, paraphrased). As our love for the Lord increases, it becomes easier for us to walk away from sin and learn to walk in integrity, trusting who we are in Him. This removes the sense of inferiority or false modesty, leaving us with only a sincere intention to please Him.

Many people think that humility is to go through life feeling like a dirty sinner. However, if we believe this, our behavior will follow. There is a time in the Christian walk when we need to transform our awareness of sin into a greater knowledge of our justification in Christ – we will live even further from sin as a result.

When I receive the truth that I am loved, justified, lovely, loyal, constant, etc. by the One who knows everything about me, I am elevated to new heights of what He thinks of me. God's thoughts towards us grant confidence to assume a healthy and whole identity.

The time has come for the Bride to be confident in what the Beloved says about her. This new stage of trust becomcs even more evident when she affirms herself:

> "I *am* the rose of Sharon, *and* the lily of the valleys. Like a lily among thorns, so is my love among the daughters."
>
> (Song of Solomon 2:1-2)

The beloved is not afraid to declare her beauty now that she has been encouraged by her beloved so many times. The rose is the most symbolic* flower, so it is as if she is saying, "I am the flower of all flowers".

The lily is a flower of simple beauty. The passage describes it as a "lily among thorns", saying that it is a delicate flower among sharp thorns. This symbolizes that the beauty of the bride is produced amid adverse situations. Even though she is surround by thorns, her beauty is even more pronounced. This speaks of the virtues that are produced in us as a result of difficult circumstances.

Enjoying the Refuge

In this stage, the bride cherishes the refreshing moments of being with the bridegroom. Now, she has been fed at his table and discovered the reality of rest and delight under the shade of the apple tree.

> The Shulamite: "Like an apple tree among the trees of the woods, *so is my beloved* among the sons. I sat down in his shade with great delight, and his fruit *was* sweet to my taste. The Shulamite to the Daughters of Jerusalem: "*He brought me* to the banqueting house, and *his banner* over me *was love.*"
>
> (Song of Solomon 2:3-4)

When the Shulamite is comparing her beloved to the apple tree, she is acknowledging the safety and relief found in him. Under the sun at noonday, she discovers a sense of protection and delight in his shade. This protection is not given as a result of our own work but because of what Jesus has done for us. The apples represent the food and satisfaction that we find in the presence of the Lord.

There is nothing more invigorating for the bride, who once worked under the harsh sun, to enjoy the safety and rest of the bridegroom's shade. Psalm 91: 1-2 says, "He who dwells in the secret place of the Most High shall abide under the shadow of the Almighty. I will say of the Lord, *He is* my refuge and my fortress; my God, in Him I will trust.".

The second moment of refreshing is when the bride once again experiences the banqueting table. She mentions the king's banner, which, in old times, referenced a symbol that would go ahead of the army guiding the way. The banner speaks of the leadership of Jesus in this scene.

When it says, "Your banner over me is love", the bride is saying that the priority of the groom is to lead her in love. In fact, the leadership of Jesus always has the goal of developing the nature of God in us, which is love. The Word says that if we fulfill the law of love, we fulfill all the laws of Christ (Romans 13:8-10).

The priority of God is not to give us physical comfort, lots of money, or power in ministry or our sphere of influence. Even though these things can be good, it is not the ultimate goal of God's work in us. Anyone can receive blessings, but not everyone can walk out the love of Christ.

The finish line for Christian maturity is a life rooted in love. Before the Lord takes us to any human achievement, He wants to lead us to the fruit of mature love. The greatest commandments are these: love God with all your heart and love your neighbor as yourself (Matthew 22:37-40). This is the banner of His leadership over us – directing us to carry out the first and second commandments.

Holy Dissatisfaction and the Hands of God

The bride begins this scene with a request, "Sustain me… because I am lovesick" (Song of Solomon 2:5). After relishing the presence of the beloved, she asks for his delicacies once again. This talks about the spiritual appetite for aspects of God's manifestation (peace, joy, refreshment etc.) that grows as we experience more of Him.

> **"The finish line for Christian maturity is a life rooted in love."**

Those who taste the presence of God no longer have the option to go back to an apathetic life. No human or fleshly experience will be as satisfying. I am used to saying that we either give ourselves fully to the desires of the flesh or we learn to live in constant spiritual hunger, reserving our appetite for the things of the Lord.

The bride says "lovesick" because she is overtaken by an unquenchable desire for the bridegroom. That is why she asks him to sustain her in this season of lovesickness. We need the "raisins" and "apples" of the Lord so we can be strengthened while we wait and yearn for His second coming. It is a holy longing that will persist until we are face to face with Jesus.

> "Sustain me with cakes of raisins, refresh me with apples, for I *am* lovesick. His left hand *is* under my head, and his right hand embraces me."
>
> (Song of Solomon 2:5-6)

The passage mentions both the right and left hands of the bridegroom. His right hand represents the visible direction of the Lord, the left hand under the bride's head, outside her line of sight, represents the invisible activity of God in our lives.

Visible leadership is when we can physically see it. They are actions that we clearly see as the hand of God moving things according to His will in us. The sovereign acts of God are around us all the time. These easily discerned movements are represented by the right hand.

The bridegroom's left hand symbolizes the imperceptible activity of God. They are actions that do not make sense at first, but are later revealed to be the hand of the Lord. Sometimes we hear people say, "Good thing the Lord kept me from marrying that person". Relationships that go wrong, for example, might be part of the invisible deliverance of God.

Even though we cannot see what the left hand is doing with the naked eye, He always makes everything work for the good of those who love Him (Romans 8:28). Sometimes we can go entire seasons without understanding the processes of the Lord, but if we remain faithful and obedient, we will see the fruit.

I tend to use the example of a tapestry being seen only from behind. When we look at it before its completion, it resembles a bunch of tangled thread, without meaning or beauty. But, once the tapestry is finished, it becomes a work of art, beautifully revealed and perfectly stitched. The processes of the Lord are like this.

Strategic Periods of God

Then, the bride says, "Do not stir up nor awaken love until it pleases" (Song of Solomon 2:7). This statement is made to the daughters of Jerusalem, who represent immature Christians. It is as if the bride is pleading with the other virgins not to hasten the romance between her and the king.

There are processes in our lives that cannot be rushed because they are ordered by God for our own maturation.

It would be wise to let the Lord dictate the seasons of our lives rather than taking control. Just like each season in the year has its own determined period, so does God's timing.

The bride then says, "Do not stir up nor awaken love until [He] pleases", meaning, do not awaken desire prematurely. When we stir up desire hastily, we become anxious and tend to violate the natural course of the maturing process. The bride wants to protect herself from arousing love too soon.

When we lived in Kansas City, while Dwayne played a number of roles at IHOP-KC (a missions base with uninterrupted 24/7 worship and prayer), there was a season in which I stayed home to take care of our small children. I had a long history of serving in ministry next to him, but at this particular moment, I could not set aside the demands of motherhood.

Seeing my dilemma, Dwayne, who has always been my biggest cheerleader, tried to intervene and open doors for me. He always stressed my qualities and encouraged me to accept new opportunities to serve in the ministry. However, I did not feel led to do so because the Lord had something else for me in that phase.

There are moments when the Lord strategically positions us in uncomfortable places to learn something. I felt like I needed that period of confinement so the Lord could minister to my heart. He was teaching me the importance of serving and loving Him through simple acts and dull routines, like changing diapers all day long. It was not glamorous, in fact it was hard and boring most of the time, but I felt the Lord wanted to teach me how to encounter him in the mundane.

If my husband, even though well-intentioned, had rushed that season in my life, I would not have learned what I needed. Dwayne even said that the Holy Spirit told him not to pressure me anymore. I felt protected by the Lord to complete that season. Clearly, the time came when I went back to being involved in the ministry. But this was only possible because I embraced that challenging season beforehand.

The bride asks, "not to awaken love", nor accelerate the process that still needs more time. We must give our stories to the Lord and be faithful in the current season, until the next one comes along. In the right moment, mature love will finally have its place.

5. Challenging the Comfort Zone

"The voice of my beloved!
Behold, he comes leaping upon the mountains…
Rise up, my love, my fair one,
And come away…
Let me see your face, let me hear your voice…
For your voice is sweet, and your face *is* lovely…
My beloved *is* mine, and I am his.
Until the day breaks and the shadows flee away,
Turn, my beloved".

Song of Solomon 2:8-17

An Invitation to Partner with the Bridegroom

In the previous season, the bride experienced delight in the presence of the bridegroom. Subsequently, she learns a new aspect of this true romance. The bridegroom introduces himself as a powerful king and calls her to an adventure with him.

> "Behold, he comes, leaping upon the mountains… Rise up, my love, my fair one, and come away…"
>
> (Song of Solomon 2:8,10)

The mountains represent the obstacles in life. By faith, we can cross mountains of difficult circumstances. In the Gospel of Mark, Jesus taught:

> "For assuredly, I say to you, whoever says to this mountain, 'Be removed and be cast into the sea,' and do not doubt in his heart, but believe that those things he says will be done, he will have whatever he says."
>
> (Mark 11:23)

The image of the bridegroom as a gazelle leaping over the mountains refers to Jesus as the sovereign King – He who triumphs (leaps) over His adversaries, human or demonic. He is not only the one who feeds her under the apple tree, he is also the valiant king that conquers the mountains.

This is a new revelation for the bride. Imagine her asking herself, "Who is this like a gazelle? I did not know that my beloved was like this!". In the same way, there are times when we are overcome by a new aspect of God that is revealed to us. We thought we had seen everything, but there are faces of the Bridegroom King that have yet to be discovered.

First, the bridegroom affirms his love for the bride, to then reveal new, more complex aspects of himself. Moreover, the progressive revelation of God is not just love, but strength, power, truth, justice, among other attributes made known to the Bride. God always takes us to new levels of understanding of who He is, unveiling new facets of His character.

When she says that "He is looking through the windows, gazing through the lattice" (Song of Solomon 2:9), the passage refers to the fact that the bridegroom is not at the banqueting hall anymore. He arose and went to the external area of the palace. He left the table of communion and is ready to start a new period in the journey between the two.

Every time that Jesus is described as "standing" in the book of Revelation, it is because He is about to do something. When He speaks to the lukewarm church, Jesus mentions standing at the door.

> "Behold, I stand at the door and knock. If anyone hears My voice and opens the door, I will come in and dine with him."
>
> (Revelation 3:20)

Then, the King exclaims, "Arise my beloved, my fair one, and come away". He, who is showing Himself as a gazelle, is calling her to leap over the mountains with Him.

The earlier phase beneath the shade of the apple tree, was sweet and comfortable, but now she is challenged to leave her comfort zone.

The bridegroom is not only the bride's place of safety, but her partner in adventure as well. While the bride only knows the place of delight with the groom, she will fall short of other important aspects of this relationship. In our walk with the Lord, there comes a time to expand our horizons and recognize various nuances of the Bridegroom's role.

"In our walk with the Lord, there comes a time to expand our horizons and recognize various nuances of the Bridegroom's role."

First, this call from the Bridegroom refers to the Great Commission. As we become the Bride of Christ, we receive the responsibility of participating in the ministry of Jesus and to do the same work that He has done – set the captives free, make disciples out of all nations, and announce the Kingdom of God (Matthew 28:19).

Second, the bridegroom's call symbolizes God leading us to unique experiences, where we are called to new levels of faith and obedience. Through the difficulties and changing seasons, our dependence on the Lord is tested. This is the stage where the bride finds herself now.

I remember a time when the Lord asked me to walk in a new level of confidence in Him. In 2012, we began to hear from the Lord about leaving the United States and moving to Brazil. We had been in Kansas City since 1998, at the International House of Prayer, and we loved everything about our lives there.

During the first decade of being married, Dwayne and I lived in different countries in Europe as young missionaries, where we also had our first daughter. We returned to the United States after living abroad for many years, so it was a huge transition for us. The city and IHOP-KC represented a phase of stability, roots, and amazing fruits. We did not have plans to leave.

But, strangely, after some time we began to feel displaced in our own city. We had a feeling that it was no longer where we were supposed to be. It did not make sense for us to feel that way because everything was going well – it could have only been something from the Lord. So, we began to fast and pray every morning for the Lord's guidance.

One morning while Dwayne and I were praying, I had a vision. In this vision, the Lord had a plant pulled from the earth in His palm, with the roots between His fingers. He then planted it in another place. I knew that this vision was about the hand of the Lord moving my family to Brazil.

Even though it was exciting, the idea of moving to a foreign nation with our three children ages 10, 13, and 16 was scary. Besides, I was over 40 years old and didn't know anyone nor speak the language. Although somewhat experienced in missionary adventures, this new endeavor required an advanced level of faith and obedience.

I waited three days before telling Dwayne this vision. Little by little the Lord began to confirm each step and gave clear signs that this was His perfect will for us. The truth is that when we come to a comfortable and predictable place, the Lord takes us to new places.

In the same way, the Bride now finds herself being challenged to leave her comfort zone. The Bridegroom says *come,* while she debates the idea of taking on the risk and adventure of something new. It is necessary for her to overcome her own fears to accept His invitation.

The Signs of the Harvest

The next line comes from the lips of the bridegroom. He is announcing the arrival of a new season. He references the song of the birds, the appearance of flowers and fruit on the trees as evidence of a new season. It is like the bridegroom is saying, "Take your eyes off yourself and look around you – observe that the harvest is coming".

This refers to the harvest of the Lord. Jesus is the Lord of the harvest, and desires that His beloved joins Him on the mission. She is a special part of His plans and purposes. It is not about the personal desires of the bride, but about the harvest that is waiting.

> "...The harvest truly *is* plentiful... Therefore, pray the Lord of the harvest to send out laborers..."
>
> (Matthew 9:37-38)

Regarding the harvest, it is one of the main ways that God calls the Bride to leave her comfort zone. Many times, it is about looking past ourselves so that we can break the cycles of complacency. For this reason, the Lord talks about the fruit that will come when she walks into uncertainty, inspiring her with a glimpse of the future.

I remember the Lord doing this with me during the process of moving to Brazil. God began to resurrect old dreams that were still in my heart. He used that moment to breathe life onto promises that I barely remembered, but were related to this new phase that was in front of us. From that moment on, I began to dream about the harvest in Brazil.

> **"Obedience becomes pleasurable when we see the coming fruit."**

Obedience becomes pleasurable when we see the coming fruit. The book of Hebrews affirms this, "…who for the joy that was set before Him [Christ] endured the cross…" (Hebrews 12:2). Even Jesus was motivated by the fruit that would come as a result of His obedience. Today, we are reaping many amazing fruits after our move to Brazil. Fruit in our own family as well as the ministry, the Lord has been extravagantly faithful in every detail.

The harvest of the Lord speaks about spiritual conquests: restoration, transformation, impact, and revival – fruit that remains in individuals and in corporate contexts. Regardless of the vision that the Lord has given us about the future, He always desires that we become part of His local and global plans.

> "For lo, the winter is past... The flowers appear on the earth."
>
> (Song of Solomon 2:11-13)

When it says, "for lo the winter is past", the bridegroom mentions that old season that the bride overcame – a long and rigorous winter. Often the Lord mentions His faithfulness in past seasons to remind us that He never ceases to intervene on our behalf. As He sustained us in the past winter, He continues to do so in every season.

The fundamental lesson in this stage of maturing is when the Bride asks, "Is the leadership of Jesus good?". Is it safe to go with Jesus even when He leads us outside our comfort zone? Does the beloved know the heart of the Bridegroom well enough to fully trust His leadership?

Even when our faith is put to the test, we discover its true quality. When we are "resting under the shade", we do not know the real limits of our fears and insecurities – these remain hidden in us. Due to the Bridegroom's love for the Bride, He challenges us to be in a place of discomfort to reveal our weaknesses, and bring forth maturity.

God confronts our self-indulgence for our own good. Everything that we have dreamed about is on the other side of our comfort zone. That which the Lord has promised as well as the harvest He has announced are only possible when we go beyond what is comfortable and familiar. God knows how to extract the maximum potential of who we can be in every aspect of our earthly trajectory.

When we trust in the Lord, we give Him license to extract the best from us. Through each process, God works to produce that which we would never be able to reach if we had led our own lives on our own strength. We do not know how to direct ourselves to the place of fulfilled promises, as that place only belongs to the Lord. Our only job is to obediently follow.

I have learned that there is no such thing as a static position on the spiritual journey. If we are not moving forward and conquering new ground in our relationship with God, then we are losing ground. As soon as we feel comfortable and begin to coast, our spiritual muscles become weak. Accordingly, the Lord is always calling us to move forward.

If we learn to exercise the muscle of our will to go beyond what is comfortable, we will reach great heights with God. In twenty, thirty, or forty years, we will continue to do greater works because we did not let our fears, or our complacent behavior stop us.

Why do what we can by our strength if the All-Powerful God is within us? When the God of all nations calls us to be His partners, with the right dose of courage and obedience, we forge ahead limitless.

The Affection of the Bridegroom Amid Fear

While the Shulamite is being challenged, the voice of her beloved continues to encourage her. Once again, he praises her loyalty, comparing her to a dove, saying:

> "O my dove, in the clefts of the rock, In the secret *places* of the cliff, let me see your face…"
>
> (Song of Solomon 2:14)

The clefts of the rock symbolize the pierced side of Jesus on the cross. The Bride takes refuge in the bruises of Christ, she is hiding in the work of His sacrifice. Moses hid in the clefts of the rock as to not be consumed by the glory of God (Exodus 33:20-22). Being hidden in Christ, through salvation, is the only way to be in the presence of the Almighty God.

The cleft of the rock is also a place of protection from the wind, where there is refuge. This refers to the secret place where we are alone with God, far from tribulation. At decisive moments, it will be even more crucial to protect ourselves from distractions and enter the Lord's presence to hear from Him.

Thus, the bridegroom asks to see his beloved's face and hear her voice. In the fight against self-indulgence, instead of feeding it, the beloved encourages her to keep calling to him. We may think that in times of crisis, our voices are repulsive and our faces ugly to Him. But the Lord never rejects a sincere heart.

It is as if God is saying, "When the time comes for new challenges, hide yourself in me and do not stop praying or worshipping. Show me your face in the place of prayer. Make your cry known to my ears in times of testing". Especially in crisis, God wants us to run to Him with confidence, instead of running from Him in condemnation.

In the next line, the bridegroom says, "Catch us the foxes, the little foxes that spoil the vines…" (Song of Solomon 2:15). The foxes that spoil the vines represent areas of compromise in the heart. Foxes are animals that seem inoffensive, but during the night they attack the vines and destroy them. Likewise, if we do not remove the foxes in our heart, they will do great damage.

> **"The Lord never rejects a sincere heart."**

In Psalm 139, the psalmist asks the Lord to search his heart to see if there is any wicked way in him. We need to examine our own hearts with the help of the Holy Spirit and remove the seeds of distraction before they become trees.

Unforgiveness begins with little unresolved offenses and isolation comes from untreated rejection. Regardless of the root of compromise, the Lord wants to heal the bride completely and deliver her from a broken and divided heart. He fully desires her, so that he may lead her to confront the obstacles under his leadership.

The Refusal of the Bride

The well-known phrase, "My beloved *is* mine, and I *am* his. He feeds *his flock* among the lilies", appears for the first time at the end of the second chapter (Song of Solomon 2:16). It is where the bride declares that she and the bridegroom belong to each other. It is not a one-sided love, as there is reciprocity and alliance.

When it mentions that he "feeds his flock by the lilies", it signifies that his leadership benefits the bride, as well as the rest of the "flock". This image refers to the Body of Christ shepherded by Jesus. The bride is recognizing the pastoral qualities of the bridegroom.

However, time goes by and she does not join her beloved in the mountains. She sends a message from afar and asks him to return before nighttime, "Until the day breaks…

Turn, my beloved, and be like a gazelle… Upon the mountains of Bether" (Song of Solomon 2:17). The word "bether" conveniently means "separation".

The bride's refusal does not indicate rebellion or outrage but immaturity and insecurity. She cannot muster the necessary courage to go with the bridegroom, so she asks him to return. The bride needs more than one day to "evaluate the invitation", but it might be too late.

6. The God that Corrects in Love

""I will rise now," *I said*,

"And go about the city…

I will seek the one I love…

I held him and would not let him go,

Until I had brought him to the house of my mother…

Of the wood of Lebanon Solomon the King

Made himself a palanquin…

And see King Solomon with the crown

With which his mother crowned him

On the day of his wedding…".

Song of Solomon 3:2-11

The Disciple of God and the Absence of the Bridegroom

In the last chapter, the bride battles her attachment to comfort, deciding to stay in her chambers while the bridegroom leapt over the mountains. When she turns down his invitation to go with him, she is alone and says, "By night on my bed I sought the one I love; I sought him, but I did not find him" (Song of Solomon 3:1).

The bride looks for her bridegroom in her bed, but he can only be found in the mountains. Even when she starts to look for him, she does it from her place of comfort. The Shulamite does not leave her room where she is safe. This attitude reflects our search for God in prayer, but we do not act outside of our own solace.

Praying is not always enough. When the Lord gives us a command, we should obey without delay. Sometimes we use the pretext that "we are praying" because we are afraid to take any action. There is a time for prayer and a time for action. In this season, the bride learns the importance of forging ahead.

The presence of the bridegroom is taken from her. This moment in the story represents the periods where we do not "feel" the presence of God as frequently. God never abandons us, and His presence is always with us. However, there are times when our sensitivity is dampened because we are in a place of ease and safety. These are phases that teach us even more about the importance of overcoming our own flesh in search of the face of God.

This chapter shows the gentle discipline of God. When the bride made an immature choice, the bridegroom responded in love, but still allowed her to feel His absence. This is a consequence of her actions as well as a learning experience. The bridegroom wants her to share in the same values as him, becoming a mature partner with similar virtues.

The Word of God tells us about divine discipline intended for good:

> "My son, do not despise the chastening of the Lord, nor be discouraged when you are rebuked by Him; for whom the Lord loves He chastens..."
>
> (Hebrews 12:5-6)

The fact that the Lord sees beauty in us despite our weaknesses does not mean that He tolerates our sin. The Lord hates sin and will do what is necessary to eliminate these areas in our lives. When God corrects us, this is not rejection. On the contrary – the discipline of the Lord qualifies us for intimacy with Him. The passage in Hebrews continues by saying:

> "...but He for *our* profit, that *we* may be partakers of His holiness."
>
> (Hebrews 12:10)

Once we become sons of God, we will not be left out of "divine education". The Word teaches us that the illegitimate son is not disciplined but the legitimate son is (Hebrews 12:7). This is not talking about a harsh and intolerant reprimand, but of a loving correction that produces maturity in the bride.

As I shared before, up to my teenage years, my parents were extremely liberal hippies. Their parenting philosophy was to put the kids in a room and let them do whatever they want – each one for his own. This is not a great environment for the youngest child with five older brothers. Let's just say that I learned to defend myself early on with punches, kicks and a sharp tongue.

My brothers and I so clearly had no limits that I lied to my friends by saying that my parents grounded me in an effort to appear normal. I would say "Oh I can't go out today, my mom grounded me". I hated the lack of parameters, I wanted to feel taken care of like the other kids.

"Discipline brings forth maximum potential. A horse has no use when it is wild and ungoverned, but the trained horse becomes valiant."

Because of this, I started to discipline myself. I gave myself rules because deep down I knew that was better for me. When

I met the Lord, I began to taste His discipline, and I was amazed. I felt loved even when He would convict me of my sins or tell me that I needed to change.

Discipline brings forth maximum potential. A horse has no use when it is wild and ungoverned, but the trained horse becomes valiant. Since God knows this, He forges us according to His virtues, acting as a patient father who persistently extracts the best from us.

It did not take long for Dwayne and I to realize the importance of correcting our small children. We believed we already knew everything, but learned so much more along the way. Raising children is hard work – but it is the worthiest job someone could have.

After hearing many depictions of family dynamics, I have noticed that most are exposed to harmful discipline. Many grow up in chaotic homes and suffer from what is called "reactionary correction" (motivated by reaction) instead of "intentional correction" which is motivated by the intention to instruct, train, and prepare a human being. Many only know of abusive discipline, which occurs when parents react aggressively, letting out their frustration on their children. Irrational discipline is the result of the mood or patience level of the parents. This kind of correction generally leaves the child insecure and confused.

Screams, aggression, and excessive punishments create fear, inferiority, and humiliation in children. This is not the godly model for discipline, it is abuse.

The investment that it takes to raise a child is 90% instruction and 10% correction. We cannot expect children to act like anything but children. We need to instruct them on how to behave, instead of just assuming they already know. I have always outlined clear expectations with my children. So, in those cases when correction was necessary, it was because they deliberately disobeyed.

When punishing them, I tried to be as calm as possible. It is never a good idea to correct children out of anger. Obviously, I have made mistakes and had several explosive moments. But when this happened, I went back and asked for my children's forgiveness, even when they were young. By the grace of God, we instilled the good values of obedience, repentance, and forgiveness.

If we can learn from our shortcomings and correct lovingly, imagine the Lord. Discipline that follows the heart of God uses minimal criticism to acquire as much learning as possible. He does not discipline out of frustration, but from love.

The Attachment to the Presence of the Bridegroom

The bride starts to literally search for him. She finally adds obedience to her prayer. She says, "I will rise now; And go about the city; In the streets and in the squares, I will seek the one I love" (Song of Solomon 3:2). She is committed to leave her chambers and find the one whom her heart loves.

Bearing in mind, it was not because of indifference or rebellion that the bride did not go, but that of immaturity. After the bridegroom's absence, she is convinced that she cannot live without him, so she is desperate to overcome the distance. Thus, she goes to the city, exposing herself to urban perils and strangers. Coming from the country as well as an inferior social class, she is unaccustomed to the challenges of a big city. This means that the bride is willing to embrace difficult and uncomfortable situations to search for her beloved. The discipline of the bridegroom begins to produce autonomy and determination in the bride.

The passage then says that the bride went to the watchmen of the city to find out about the groom's whereabouts.

> "Have you seen the one I love?"
>
> (Song of Solomon 3:3)

As we saw in the introduction, the watchmen represent the leaders in the church or more experienced Christians with spiritual authority. It is pertinent to seek news from the guards as she longs for her intimacy with the king.

In the same way, there are times when we must run to more mature Christians so they can redirect us to Jesus. We need one another to gain strengthen because we are not self-sufficient. As the scriptures say:

> "Two are better than one... If either of them falls down, one can help the other up."
>
> (Ecclesiastes 4:9-10)

The passage continues, "Scarcely had I passed by them, when I found the one I love..." (Song of Solomon 3:4). As soon as the bride leaves the guards, she finds her beloved. The period of his absence was not long, because he quickly rewards her act of obedience. This takes us to another related passage.

> "For everyone who asks receives; the one who seeks finds; and to the one who knocks, the door will be opened."
>
> (Matthew 7:8)

The bridegroom has no pleasure in a prolonged reprimand. As soon as the young woman leaves her comfort zone, she is rewarded for her obedience. In the same way, God knows the sincerity of our hearts instead of highlighting our errors, He celebrates our triumphs. The book of Hebrews says that the Lord rewards those who earnestly seek Him (Hebrews 11:6).

> **"For many, it is harder to testify about Jesus in our own homes than anywhere else. Our closest family members have a unique ability to provoke strong emotions and remind us of our past."**

The bride also says, "…I held him and would not let him go, Until I had brought him to the house of my mother…" (Song of Solomon 3:4). After experiencing a period without her beloved, the bride holds onto him with even more strength and gratefulness than ever. She no longer takes his closeness for granted. His presence becomes precious to her.

She says, "I had brought him to the house of my mother", which signifies inviting Jesus to our familiar places. When we take the context of the gospel to our friends and family, we are unashamed to take ownership of our faith in Christ in front of those who are close to us. The more precious He becomes to us, the more confident we are to introduce Him to people.

For many, it is harder to testify about Jesus in our own homes than anywhere else. Our closest family members have a unique ability to provoke strong emotions and remind us of our past. When we walk out transformation, they are the first to test the authenticity of our change and hold us to who we were in the past.

Introducing Dwayne to my family was interesting from the get-go. I preferred not to let my two worlds collide. My family was a little crazy in both good and bad ways. Conversely, Dwayne's ideal Christian family looked like they could grace the cover of a homeschool magazine. His parents were pastors, read the Bible, and raised their children in the principles of the Lord from a young age. The first time that I took Dwayne to meet my family, my brothers literally put him in a headlock.

Lalk about a clash of family cultures! Believe me when I say that I am grateful for my family and the crazy way I was raised. It produced a grit in me that the Lord has redeemed.

Still, it is important for her to take the bridegroom to her mother's house. She is open to introducing the king to her modest family of rural workers, maybe where he will not be well understood. In spite of the risks, she now has the courage to bring him to her most familiar place.

Jesus as the Safe Savior

In the next verse, the Shulamite will see the king coming out of the wilderness, surrounded by merchant's spices and his valiant men. The king's arrival is announced by "Who is this". The announcer of this phrase, although unknown in the story, represents the Holy Spirit. He is the one who points to Jesus and reveals Him to the world.

> "Who *is* this coming out of the wilderness…
>
> And see King Solomon with the crown
>
> With which his mother crowned him
>
> On the day of his wedding…"
>
> (Song of Solomon 3:6,11)

This moment refers to Jesus' triumph as the Savior that overcame the wilderness through His crucifixion. The "coming out of the wilderness" refers to the ascension of Christ when He arose to Heaven after the resurrection. The clouds of smoke refer to the glory and majesty of the Son of God when raised from the dead. He is the "firstborn from the dead" that rose in glory.

The mention of myrrh, the burial balm, points to the death of Jesus, as mentioned earlier. The incense refers to Christ's intercession before the Father.

> "...*It is* Christ who died, and furthermore is also risen, who is even at the right hand of God, who also makes intercession for us."
>
> (Romans 8:34)

The passage goes on, "Behold, it *is* Solomon's carriage, *with* sixty valiant men around it, of the valiant of Israel" (Song of Solomon 3:7). The carriage of Solomon was a chariot* made from precious materials used to transport the king. This image refers to the throne where Jesus sits in Heaven. The Word says that "... We do have such a high priest, who sits at the right hand of the throne of the Majesty in heaven" (Hebrews 8:1).

These valiant men denote a powerful protection system around the king. This represents how Jesus is clothed with all authority against the power of darkness. He is the undefeated King that took the keys of death and hell (Revelation 1:18). Crushing the head of the serpent and sending us to do the same.

The valiant men and experts in war symbolize the Holy Spirit experience that protects and saves us from the enemy's pitfalls. He knows every evil scheme and how to rescue us from all of them. Maybe He uses a dream to alert us or raises up people to intercede for us – regardless of how He does it, the Holy Spirit keeps us from harm. This image also refers to the spiritual escort of the Bride of Christ. We are not impotent and inoperative, but the triumphant Church of Christ.

In Matthew 16, Jesus affirms that the gates of hell will not prevail against the Church. The beloved here is becoming more and more conscious of her authority and divine protection as she becomes the Bride of Christ.

The passage mentions that it was King Solomon himself who made the carriage. This speaks of the realization that Christ seized the position of authority over all kingdoms of this world in His obedience. He conquered the throne at the right hand of the Father and makes us sit with Him in heavenly places (Ephesians 2:6). The wood of Lebanon signifies strength and beauty, the silver represents redemption, and the gold symbolizes divine character.

The bride calls the daughters of Jerusalem to see the bridegroom crowned by his mother. As an invitation, she says, "And see King Solomon with the crown with which his mother crowned him on the day of his wedding" (Song of Solomon 3:11). This crown represents the bridegroom's achievement of leading the bride into mature love. At the wedding of the Lamb, the bridegroom has the joy of preparing for Himself a glorious Bride (Revelation 19:7).

Since the bride has not concluded her journey into maturity, the wedding has not yet arrived. It is as if she has a prophetic foreshadowing of her wedding day with the bridegroom-king. She sees the end of the story and the celebration that is waiting – she feels hopeful and ecstatic.

It is in the same way that we wait for the second coming of Christ and hold onto the promises of the Marriage of the Lamb with great excitement. Even if we suffer tribulations, we live with the expectation of finishing our love story with King Jesus. The glimpse of an eternal future with Christ feeds our hope and sustains our heart.

7. The Ravished Heart of God

“Behold, you *are* fair, my love!
Behold, you *are* fair!...
Until the day breaks and the shadows flee away,
I will go my way to the mountain of myrrh
And to the hill of frankincense…
You have ravished my heart, my sister, *my* spouse…
A fountain of gardens, a well of living waters,
And streams from Lebanon.
Awake, O north *wind*, and come, O south!”

Song of Solomon 4:1-16

The Budding Virtues

As we read in the last chapter, the bride takes her first steps of obedience. She tastes the absence of the bridegroom and learns to go beyond what is comfortable, to unknown places. The beloved went to the big city but did not join her beloved in the mountain of obstacles.

The next chapter of the story is about one of the characteristics of God that I love and respect most. He is a God that can see the virtues that are still hidden within us. Our creator searches our inner man and sees qualities that have not come forth yet but are about to flourish.

> "Behold, you *are* fair, my love! Behold, you *are* fair!"
>
> (Song of Solomon 4:1)

In this new stage of the real romance, this attribute of God will show how the bridegroom begins speaking new qualities over the bride. He becomes even more detailed in how he highlights the virtues that are budding in his beloved. Once again, she is consoled by loving affirmations from the bridegroom king.

The Word says that God calls those things which do not exist as though they do (Romans 4:17). With the creative power of His words, God brings forth what has not yet manifested, including the small virtues that are hidden within us. The more that the bridegroom declares the bride's virtues, the more virtuous she becomes, making herself a bride who is ready.

Jesus nourishes His Bride and washes her with His words. As it says in Ephesians:

> "...that He might sanctify and cleanse her with the washing of water by the word, that He might present her to Himself a glorious church... For no one ever hated his own flesh, but nourishes and cherishes it, just as the Lord *does* the church."
>
> (Ephesians 5:26-29)

In the first part, the bridegroom is going to speak eight affirmations over the bride. Even though these characteristics are not fully formed in the bride yet, they are still found inside her. As expected, each one of these attributes also refers to a symbolic correspondence to the virtues that Jesus is producing in the Church.

The first attribute is about the eyes of the bride, which he compares to doves. Once again, this speaks about loyalty and devotion. Even though the bride faltered in her devotion to the bridegroom in the earlier phase, he still considers her loyalty to him, because he sees her sincere heart.

He also compares her hair to goat hair, which indicates dedication. Teeth like a flock of shorn sheep refer to the ability of the Bride to chew on the Word. She is learning to go to solid food, because milk is for babies in the faith (Hebrews 5:13).

Notice that the language in these descriptions use images from rural life. The Shulamite was a peasant and knew the agricultural and livestock aspects of which the groom is speaking. He does not use difficult or distant terms, but those that are familiar to her, from the setting of her daily life.

God loves to communicate truth to our hearts in specific and intimate ways. Only He knows us completely and can describe who we are with precision. He is the one who gave each of us our unique identity when creating our personality, temperament, skills, and talents according to what He desired.

> **"God loves to communicate truth to our hearts in specific and intimate ways. Only He knows us completely and can describe who we are with precision."**

When Dwayne and I had children, we quickly learned how different they are. Our girls, Sydney and Chloe, had very different personalities and interests from the beginning. While Sydney loved to play with a karaoke microphone and pretend to sing and preach to the multitudes, Chloe would make us sit at the dinner table and play "business meeting".

It is impressive how children, early on, manifest their personality when they are given an opportunity to be free and enjoyed for who they are. As parents, we wanted to optimize the uniqueness in each of our children, so we asked the Lord "Who are they in Your eyes?". We began to ask for divine wisdom to raise them the way the Lord intended.

God loves our differences, which is why He Himself created us exactly as we are. He made us uniquely and perfectly equipped for our life purpose.

> "For You formed my inward parts; You covered me in my mother's womb. I will praise You, for I am fearfully *and* wonderfully made; marvelous are Your works, and *that* my soul knows very well."
>
> (Psalm 139:13-14)

The next characteristic mentioned is the bride's lips. Her lips like the color of scarlet, like that of the blood of Jesus, representing lips that make declarations of redemption. The bride is exchanging slander for a speech that carries divine perspective.

The king compliments the kisses of the beloved, corresponding to the kisses of the Word that we receive from God, the revelation of the scriptures in the secret place. The bridegroom also mentions the faces of the bride behind the veil, symbolizing expressed emotions. The beloved is learning how to convey healthy emotions under the leadership of the beloved.

The king compares her neck to the tower of David. The neck and its ability to turn the head speaks of submission. Hence, the eighth and last attribute are the breasts compared to two fawns. The breasts evoke breastfeeding and the capacity to nurture. This signifies a new season of maturity where she is able to give spiritual milk to those who are young and immature.

These eight characteristics are little sprouts of virtues in the bride that the bridegroom-King can already see as if they had bloomed. The investments that he has made in the beloved will surely bear fruit, so he treats her as such. God's capacity to relate to us as if we were already the final product of our processes is what is called "the prophetic heart of God".

Instead of pointing out our weaknesses and making us even more aware of them, God talks about our virtues and calls them forth. When Gideon was hiding in the mill afraid of the Midianite army, the Lord called him valiant (Judges 6:12). How amazing is God's perspective? He is saying, "You are much better than your current behavior".

God sees our entire life and relates to us through the lens of who we will be in our maturity. He does not define us based on a few moments of cowardice, doubt, and immaturity, but according to His eternal gaze. Even in our mistakes, it is His kindness that leads us to repentance (Romans 2:4).

Every time we feel condemnation because of our failures, it does not come from God, but rather from the enemy (Revelation 12:10). The accuser puts our knowledge about the character of God to the test. If we do not know that He is good, long-suffering, and forgiving, the enemy tells us that He is angry, disappointed and frustrated with us.

These lies are overcome by the power of truth. The daily spiritual battle happens in the battlefield of the mind through what we believe by exchanging our own ideas of God with the truth of the Bible. When we listen to the voice of the enemy, he gains territory. When we mold what we believe around the truths of God's character, the enemy and his imprisoning lies lose ground in our lives.

Deciding to Go up the Mountain

In Song of Solomon 4, we observe the Shulamite declaring that she will go to the mountains for the first time. After she went to the big city looking for her beloved, she is willing to answer his initial call to join him in the mountain of obstacles. She declares:

> "Until the day breaks, and the shadows flee away, I will go my way to the mountain of myrrh, and to the hill of frankincense."
>
> (Song of Solomon 4:6)

Once again, the myrrh reappears in the story as a symbol of death and sacrifice. It is as if the bride was saying that she is willing to go up the mountain of sacrifice, where her beloved also surrendered himself. This is a metaphor of the willingness of the Church to enter the suffering of Christ, as in "For to this you were called, because Christ also suffered for us, leaving us an example, that you should follow His steps" (1 Peter 2:21).

The hill of incense represents the place of intercession. The bride commits herself to engage in prayer and search for the bridegroom. The more she dedicates herself to intercession, the more strengthened she is to climb the hill of sacrifice. In the same way, the Lord equips us in prayer and devotion to live sacrificially for His purposes.

The king then says, "Come with me from Lebanon, *my* spouse… Look from the top of Amana, from the top of Senir and Hermon, from the lions' dens, from the mountains of the leopards" (Song of Solomon 4:8). Not only does he invite her to go with him, but he says that there are lions and leopards where he is. This means that the Bride will go through spiritual battles, but will come out victorious, because she is committed to intercession.

In response to the devotion of the bride, the king says, "And *there is* no spot in you" (Song of Solomon 4:7). There is no spot in her? Did he forget how challenging it was for her to overcome the attachment to comfort? Surely not. But, once again, the commitment of the bridegroom to shower her in words of love and dignity leads him to highlight her virtues instead of her failures.

In Hebrews 11, Abraham is described as someone who did not waver in the faith. And I wonder, "Are you sure he did not waver?". He conceived an illegitimate child with Agar trying to speed up the fulfillment of the promise. Yet, in the end of the story, he is seen as an example of heroism because he persevered in faith.

We also know the story of David. At a certain moment of his life, he was a murderer and adulterer, but this was not the story that God told in the Bible. Because of his contrite heart, David is cited in the faith hall of fame and in many other biblical records as one of the most relevant men for fulfilling God's promises throughout the course of history.

> **"The commitment of the bridegroom to shower her in words of love and dignity leads him to highlight her virtues instead of her failures."**

I love the "editing" process of God. The way that He tells our story is completely different from how we tell it. If we could hear Him narrating our story, I think we would be surprised. The plot would not be full of mistakes and defects, as we would think, but it would celebrate our personal victories and our steps of faith.

If you look at your current condition and feel paralyzed by your failures, remember the "divine editing process" is in your favor. The imperfect stories of the Bible unfold in the most improbable ways so that the glory belongs only to the Lord. Psalms 34:5 says that if we look to Him, we will not be ashamed.

The Ravished Heart of God

Consequently, the bridegroom makes a declaration that refers to the deep desire that Jesus has for the Bride. She says, "You have ravished my heart… With one *look* of your eyes, with one link of your necklace" (Song of Solomon 4:9). The king reveals his ravished heart for the bride. Without much effort, with just one look, he feels consumed with tenderness and admiration for her.

This expresses the intense passion of Christ for the Church, as in the passion between husband and wife. Paul says:

> "For this reason a man shall leave his father and mother and be joined to his wife, and the two shall become one flesh." This is a great mystery, but I speak concerning Christ and the church."
>
> (Ephesians 5:31-32)

Jesus has a deep affection for us. John 15:9 says, "As the Father loved Me, I also have loved you…". This means that we are loved with an intense unconditional love, which we received freely through Christ. He desires to reveal His heart full of tenderness and passion for us.

For a long time, theologians and philosophers debated the legitimate idea of a God that has emotions for his people. The Greeks believed that God could not have feelings for us because it would make him vulnerable to humanity. However, the Bible's Christian paradigm depicts a God that is involved in human affairs.

He loved us so much that he became one of us, taking on human form and expressing the loftiest form of love, which is to die for another. When the offering of love from Jesus corresponds to a Bride willing to give her life and submit to the maturing process, the Bridegroom's heart is overtaken by tenderness.

If Christ loved us when we were sinners and by all appearances, His enemies, imagine His delight when we learn to respond to His love with obedience? It is an excessive love. He is consumed with passion for his bride simply by one look of her eyes. The eyes are known as the windows to the soul, but they also represent the heart.

The Lord knows every movement of our heart. He notices the simplest, most subtle gesture of love. Do we know our capacity to move the heart of God with our silent decisions to love Him? The Lord sees our intentions and never misinterprets them. People can misjudge us, but Jesus sees even the slightest movement of our heart towards him. No one will ever love us as extravagantly as the Lord does.

The passage also says that he is ravished "with one link of your necklace". As mentioned before, the neck refers to submission to the Lord. The necklace around her neck represents every personal decision to submit to God's processes and every act of obedience. This journey is made up of these small choices to bow to His leadership.

When Dwayne and I moved back to the United States, after living ten years as missionaries, I confess that I felt like a failure. I could not see the fruit of all those years of service. Returning to our home country exhausted without tangible results seemed to be the height of defeat. I remember feeling crushed and asking God to erase all those years and let me start over. I felt like I had labored in my own strength and burned out.

During that time, I remember reading this passage in Song of Solomon and the Lord ministered to my heart. He told me that our obedience was not in vain after all those years. Every act of service in the mission field ravished the heart of God, it didn't matter if I could see the fruit or not. I cried so hard when the Lord gave me His perspective of our time in missions. As I was weeping, I said to the Lord through my tears, "You mean my labor meant something to You even if it was done with a wrong attitude?" Our "necklaces" of submission ravish the heart of God. Keep in mind that He is the God that recalls even a cup of water given in His name. I am undone by His generous assessment of our love and labor in His name. God's kindness is extremely apparent, as in, "For God is not unjust to forget your work and labor of love which you have shown toward his name, in that you have ministered to the saints and do minister" (Hebrews 6:10).

Then, the king calls her "my sister", which refers to the quality of being known in our humanity. Jesus took on human flesh and shared the human experience, although He is fully God. That is mind blowing in and of itself, let alone that he would choose humanity as His bride. He lived in our midst and had natural human experiences and faced temptation just as we have, and yet never sinned. He is a great high priest who is sympathetic in all His ways. He is saying, "You are like me. I know the weaknesses that you face". He understands our mortality, not just because he created us, for He came to Earth and lived among us as a man. He is acquainted with all our ways, up close and personally. This truth alone makes me love Jesus. I believe we will forever be in awe of the cross and the fact that Jesus is GOD yet laid aside His glory to buy us back. When we see Him in all of His splendor, we will begin to understand what a great sacrifice He made to lower Himself to human form so that he could exalt us to a position of privilege as His Bride.

When I think about how Jesus understands all my humanness and still loves me, I am overcome by fascination. How is it possible that He knows every one of my weaknesses? When a stranger or acquaintance says, "I love you", this phrase has no effect. Love is proven genuine when it remains, despite the knowledge of our imperfections.

One time, Dwayne and I were leading a team of young adult missionaries on a three-month trip to India. In the training before the trip, some of them came to me and said, "We love you Jennifer!". Even though I felt flattered, I thought to myself, "Let's wait for the end of the trip to see if you really love me".

During the intense schedule, I was sleep deprived and bombarded with daily challenges, as a result, I was not always the best version of myself. Quite the opposite really, so that team saw many of my defects. Yet, at the end of it all, they said, "We love you Jennifer", which deeply moved me.

The bridegroom says that her love is better than wine. He is developing the line from the beginning when the bride affirms the same phrase. He also mentions the fragrance of the bride, which takes us back to the first compliments that the bride gave him.

The fragrance speaks of the aroma of our inner life. The more we cultivate intimacy with God, the more we are filled with His essence. The bridegroom mentions the honey on the lips of his beloved, which represents the words of worship and prayer that flow from the bride.

He says, "A garden enclosed *is* my sister…" (Song of Solomon 4:12). The enclosed garden signifies the purity and exclusivity of the bride with the bridegroom. Only the royalty could have an enclosed garden at that time, as it was a symbol of enjoyment and rest. The reward of the king was to rest in his private garden. In the same way, Jesus' reward is to enjoy intimacy with us.

The cited spices of spikenard and saffron, calamus and cinnamon, myrrh and aloes refer to enjoyment and delight as well. There is no "frugality" in the place of intimacy, only abundance, so counting the cost is unnecessary. The passage says she is like, "A spring shut up, a fountain sealed" (Song of Solomon 4:15), that is, it is as crystalline waters that flow from the springs. The groom is saying that for him, she is pure and immaculate.

Crying for the Winds of Change

Finally, the Shulamite makes a declaration, "Awake, O north *wind,* and come, O south!" (Song of Solomon 4:16). She is asking that the winds blow in her garden and spread its aromas. Or in other words, she is surrendering to the leadership of Jesus, knowing that many times His ways are not her own.

The north wind represents adversity and the south wind represents blessings. The Bride is mature and confident in God's lovingkindness enough to ask Him to send the winds of change. She knows that both the wind of testing and the wind of blessing will help her grow in a deeper level of love and maturity.

This is a decisive moment in the story because it represents a mark of maturity for the Bride. She is so aware of the benefits of God's discipline that she requests it. She is not afraid to beckon the winds of testing, because she knows that both the north and south winds are necessary for her to become a fragrant garden or mature in love.

Similarly, we learn to love the processes of God in us. Not only spring produces the harvest, but all the seasons with their characteristics. The right amount of both testing and blessing produces the precise condition for the fruit to come forth. In other words, the bride is asking the beloved to send blessings as well as testing, to refine and mature her love.

She then says, "Let my beloved come to his garden and eat its pleasant fruits" (Song of Solomon 4:16), meaning that the bridegroom would enjoy the fruits of maturity that he produced in his inner man. Starting from this declaration, the next chapters of Song of Solomon focus on the treasures that the bridegroom finds in the bride, rather than those she finds in him.

The beloved is ready to embrace the upcoming progression and become a bride that is more and more willing to enter partnership with the bridegroom. The journey takes her to even higher places, as her obedience captured the heart of the beloved.

8. The Two-Fold Test

"I have come to my garden, *my* sister, my spouse;
I have gathered my myrrh with my spice…
I opened for my beloved, but my beloved had turned away *and* was gone…
The watchmen who went about the city found me.
They struck me, they wounded me… My beloved…
Chief among ten thousand. Turn your eyes away from me,
for they have overcome me….
Who is she who looks forth as the morning?"

Song of Solomon 5:1-12, 6:5-10

The Communion of Suffering

The last chapter ends with a prayer from the bride. After being complimented by the king for her budding virtues, the beloved feels confident enough to ask for the winds of testing, because she understands that they are necessary for the fragrance of her garden to spread.

> "I have come to my garden, my sister, *my* spouse;
> I have gathered my myrrh with my spice;
> I have eaten my honeycomb with my honey;
> I have drunk my wine with my milk..."
>
> (Song of Solomon 5:1)

A new phrase starts with "I have come to my garden, my sister". The bridegroom begins with the affirmation that he will go into her garden to enjoy the myrrh, balm, honey, wine, and milk. These elements represent the inheritance of Jesus, the enclosed garden represents the Bride. She becomes his exclusive possession when she chooses the way of devotion and complete surrender.

1 Peter 2:9 says we are "…His own special people…". It is not only the bride who has an inheritance by joining the bridegroom, but He also enjoys an inheritance by having us as His possession. The next line says, "Eat, O friends! Drink, yes, drink deeply…". This represents the Jesus' invitation to the entire Body of Christ to enjoy the fruits of maturity that He produced in us.

Then, the bride says, "I sleep, but my heart is awake; *It is* the voice of my beloved! ..." (Song of Solomon 5:2). While she is watching and waiting in her bed, she is visited by him, knocking on the door. Revelation 3 says:

> "Behold, I stand at the door and knock. If anyone hears My voice and opens the door, I will come in and dine with him, and he with Me."
>
> (Revelation 3:20)

The passage says the bride finds herself outside, her hair covered with dew and the drops of the night. This is a representation of Jesus as the one who endured the dark and lonely night in Gethsemane before going to the cross, as He was sweating drops of blood and surrendering His will to the Father (Luke 22:42-44).

The bridegroom is calling her to join in his sufferings. Since she asked to be tested, he appears at her door to answer her prayer. The Word says:

> "...but rejoice to the extent that you partake of Christ's sufferings, that when His glory is revealed, you may also be glad with exceeding joy."
>
> (1 Peter 4:13)

The subject of participating in the sufferings of Christ is not a popular one among Christians. People generally prefer to know about how to use faith to get a new car, a house, or a boyfriend instead of asking how to take part in Jesus' suffering. However, this is an important aspect of Christianity.

Jesus learned to obey through suffering (Hebrews 5:8). He told His disciples:

> "If anyone desires to come after Me, let him deny himself, and take up his cross daily, and follow Me. For whoever desires to save his life will lose it, but whoever loses his life for My sake will save it."
>
> (Luke 9:23-24)

Christian suffering is also connected to the abdication of things that compete for our love for God. Bearing in mind, the goal of the Lord is to lead us to the first commandment, which is to love Him above all else. The Lord knows that we must learn how to die to our old nature.

In Colossians 3:5, we are counseled to put to death all that belongs to our earthly nature. The processes that lead us to holiness are not pleasurable in themselves but produce the desired outcome. The exercises that make a muscle strong are the same ones that make our muscles become very sore as they are being stretched.

> "My brethren, count it all joy when you fall into various trials, knowing that the testing of your faith produces patience."
>
> (James 1:2-3)

It seems crazy to think that we should find joy in the testing. However, the Bible says this is how we produce virtues as perseverance.

Another aspect of biblical suffering is related to persecution for the sake of Christ. There are countless biblical references to suffering for doing good.

> "Blessed are you when people insult you, persecute you and falsely say all kinds of evil against you because of me. Rejoice and be glad, because great is your reward in heaven, for in the same way they persecuted the prophets who were before you."
>
> (Matthew 5:11-12)

> "For it has been granted to you on behalf of Christ not only to believe in him, but also to suffer for him."
>
> (Philippians 1:29)

In these verses, it is evident that there is a biblical suffering ordained for the glory of God through us. This is the stage that the bride is about to walk into. She responds to the visit of the bridegroom by saying, "I have taken off my robe; How can I put it on *again?* I have washed my feet; How can I defile them?" (Song of Solomon 5:3). Even though this passage has caused controversy among theologians, the bride is not refusing to open the door out of rebellion. Quite the opposite, it can be paraphrased as, "Now that I have removed my old nature, should I put it on again?".

The phrase "I have washed my feet" also refers to being washed by the Word and not wanting to return to our old ways of living. The bride does not want to dirty herself again with her own self-righteousness as she prefers to keep her justification with Jesus. This vision is confirmed when she shudders upon seeing the bridegroom running his hand through the crack in the door. Her shudder represents fear and reverence, not rebellion.

When she rises to open the door, her fingers are dripping in myrrh. Once again, this balm references her willingness to embrace suffering. The bride is being anointed with the perfume of obedience because she has been chosen to enter the suffering of the bridegroom. After she makes this choice, the testing comes.

The Two-Fold test

The Shulamite opens the door for her beloved, but he is not there. She says, "I sought him, but I could not find him; I called him, but he gave me no answer" (Song of Solomon 5:6). The bride's soul weakens as she finds herself alone again. For the second time, the bridegroom's presence is taken from her, but this time the motive is not disobedience.

While the first absence of the groom took place to correct the bride's desire for comfort, this second moment represents a seal of approval for her mature obedience. It seems contradictory that she would be rewarded for her obedience with another period of testing. However, this is not an uncommon theme in the Bible. After Joseph demonstrated obedience to God, he was thrown into prison twice (Genesis 37-50). Even though David walked in the approval of the Lord, he went through a long period of persecution and discouragement (1 Samuel 20-21). These men were not undergoing discipline for making concessions, but were tested due to their great callings.

The Word of the Lord says that the one who has fruit is pruned by the Father. Jesus said that every branch, in Him, that does not give fruit He cuts, and every branch that gives fruit He prunes, so that it gives more fruit (John 15:2). Even though cutting and pruning seem the same, cutting eliminates forever and pruning cuts temporarily so that further growth is even greater.

We had neighbors in the United States that pruned their trees. One time I was watching as their tree was pruned down to just a trunk and two twigs. I thought they had destroyed the tree, with no chance of producing anything again. To my surprise, after a long, ugly winter, the leaves on the tree began to grow back.

"A mature Bride must obtain the essential nutrients from the immutable Word of God, not from her emotions."

It is in the winter season that the roots of the trees go deep. The nutrients that were found on the surface are no longer there, so a deeper layer of soil is required to feed and survive. In this process, the tree nourishes its roots system and never goes back to the previous one.

This is the same way that I see the period of God's "absence". He removes the superficial nutrients so that we can go deeper. The Lord is not abandoning us, because He promised that He would never forsake us (Hebrews 13:5). Nonetheless, some of the ease of His manifested presence is taken away so that we learn to take root in the soil of the Word.

When we adapt to the presence of God, we tend to be led by our emotions. However, the truth about who God is does not reside in what we feel, it occurred even before we existed or felt anything. A mature Bride must obtain the essential nutrients from the immutable Word of God, not her emotions.

Subsequently, the Shulamite is faced with the second test. The passage says, "The watchmen who went about the city found me. They struck me, they wounded me… Took my veil away from me" (Song of Solomon 5:7). The watchmen that helped her before, now hurt her. They represent the spiritual leaders that possess the power to grant or revoke a role or function of authority. When they remove her veil, it means they are depriving her of carrying out her ministry.

Conjuring up a negative idea about pastors and leaders is not my intention. Dwayne and I have been in ministry for years, and we still are. As leaders, we have made so many mistakes amid our victories. As church members, we have seen the Lord intentionally use our leaders to shake our ministerial stability and test our hearts.

Personally, I have gone through a period that combined both the silence of God and ministerial deprivation – a two-fold test. At a church service in Kansas City, I had a vision of myself running in an Olympic stadium when, all of a sudden, the Lord took me out of the race and sent me to the bleachers. I asked, "Lord, why did you take me out? I was running!". The Lord responded, "Jennifer, are you able to grow in the dark?". This question shook me to my core because I knew He was asking me something serious. So, I said, "Yes Lord, I am able to grow in the dark.". Then, I had the immediate sensation that a concrete wall had been erected between us and I could no longer feel His presence.

In the first months, I felt desperate when I could not sense the Lord's presence. In the prayer room at IHOP-KC, it was as if a bubble prevented me from being touched by that atmosphere. I could be in the most "anointed" place imaginable, but unable to feel the presence of God.

In an attempt to fix this situation, I started to confess all the sins that came to mind – my sins, my parents' sins, my distant relatives' sins. I did not know what was wrong with me. Feeling confused and rejected, I just wanted to put an end to the distance.

In the area of ministry, I felt invisible as well. Even though I already had years of experience ministering the Word, all my influence seemed to have been taken away. As Dwayne was always preaching and ministering, people just assumed I was with him. But I was hidden, waiting for the Lord to break His silence and restore His presence.

In this phase, wherever I went, people would give me prophetic words saying, "The Lord says you are not alone. He sees you.", and I would think *Why doesn't He come and tell me this directly?!* At that moment, it dawned on me that God was not rejecting or discipling me, He was hiding me so that my roots would go deep in His undeniable truths.

It was a long period where the Lord only spoke to me through burdens of intercession. I would read the Bible, but it was dry. I remember saying to the Lord, "Even if you never personally speak to me again, you are still good". Nothing about the Lord and who He is had changed, He was still worthy and true. I felt the activity of the Holy Spirit around me when I would intercede, but I didn't feel the personal connection I had always valued. However, the firmness in the Word that I acquired in those years has been the foundation of my life ever since. That particular season brought stability and broke my addiction to my emotions. My roots went deep in that season and I found treasures in the dark, so to speak. I am grateful for what the Lord produced in me, which will never be taken away.

An expression that has been used to describe this phase is *the dark night of the soul.* I read that Mother Theresa experienced the *dark night of the soul* for 50 years, which is intense! My season did not last decades, but it was long enough for my frame.

This is the moment in time that the bride finds herself. She was the one who wanted to grow in maturity. How many of us have prayed: "Lord I want to grow! I want to love you more!"? He responds to our prayers by sending the winds of change. The Bride will learn to bear the distance while keeping her heart loyal to the Bridegroom, as her love is maturing.

The Mature Response to Testing

The winds of adversity came in the form of a two-fold test to prove the bride's love. She was alone without her veil of authority (ministry). Trials like these come to test the quality of our obedience. Likewise, fire is the only requirement to verify if the gold is truly pure or simply a mix of metals.

The trials of fire come to prove that we are truly faithful, perseverant, and trusting God. The apostle Peter wrote:

> "Beloved, do not think it strange concerning the fiery trial which is to try you, as though some strange thing happened to you; but rejoice to the extent that you partake of Christ's sufferings, that when His glory is revealed, you may also be glad with exceeding joy."
>
> (1 Peter 4:12-13)

In response to the two-fold test that she endured, the bride says, "I charge you, O daughters of Jerusalem, If you find my beloved, That you tell him I *am* lovesick!" (Song of Solomon 5:7). The reaction of the bride is shocking, as she reveals a heart free of offense. Instead of showing resentment, she is even more in love with the bridegroom.

"The trials of fire come to prove that we are truly faithful, perseverant, and trusting God."

That young immature woman, who preferred to stay comfortable in her bed, is now wisely responding to the challenges. Even though she has been wounded by the watchman and suffered from the absence of her beloved, she responds in humility and purity. She does not let bitterness penetrate her heart, she continues to love the bridegroom, without blaming him for what happened. In Matthew 11:6, Jesus says blessed is he who is not offended because of Me.

God also tested Job by letting the enemy touch several areas of his life, demonstrating that he would remain faithful even after losing everything. Job's reason for loving the Lord was not because of His blessings, but for who He is. Job's response was complete obedience.

> "In all this Job did not sin nor charge God with wrong."
>
> (Job 1:22)

There is nothing more beautiful to the Lord than an unoffended heart towards Him. No blessing or miracle that the Lord can give us will ever compare to the beauty of a heart that trusts the Lord, even when the blessings do not come. This is the kind of devotion that testing produces.

The loyalty of the bride is so amazing that it intrigues the daughters of Jerusalem. As aforementioned, they represent immature, but sincere Christians. They ask, "What *is* your beloved, More than *another* beloved… That you so charge us?" (Song of Solomon 5:9), another way of saying it is "what is so special about him that you remain loyal?" or "why do you love him so much after what he did?"

The daughters of Jerusalem refer to "another beloved", which represents their other loves, since they are still immature. The substitute pleasures that immature Christians have are things like money, comfort, power, ministry, recreation, other people, etc. Sincere Christians, in their immaturity, can love these things more than Jesus.

In response to the question of the daughters of Jerusalem, the bride describes the virtues of the bridegroom. Her declarations demonstrate her knowledge of the one she is loyal to. Her heart is rooted in the truths of who he is. Besides, her commitment is not based on what she feels, but what she knows to be true about him.

The beloved starts by saying, "…Chief among ten thousand…" (v. 10). This means there is no one like him. His head like refined gold represents the perfect and sovereign leadership of Jesus. His wavy locks and eyes like doves speak of His dedication and loyalty to the Church.

As in the language used to describe the bride's virtues, the face refers to the groom's emotions. She is saying, "See how lovely the bridegroom's emotions are for me!" She mentions the hands, body, and legs of the beloved, which represent the purposes of God in action. All these references point to the divine qualities of Jesus.

She finally says, "His mouth *is* most sweet, yes, he *is* altogether lovely. This *is* my beloved, and this *is* my friend" (Song of Solomon 5:16). He is the one she identifies as a friend, partner, and neighbor. They have grown in intimacy and now carry similar virtues. Jesus said, "No longer do I call you servants, ...but I have called you friends..." (John 15:15).

When they hear the attributes of the bridegroom, the daughters of Jerusalem ask the Shulamite where he is. In other words, they also want to have an encounter with the king. This is the effect that we have when we demonstrate legitimate intimacy with Jesus. The people around us say, "Where can I find Him too?"

Breaking the Silence

A new cycle begins when the bridegroom breaks the silence by complimenting the bride for her mature response to the testing. He could barely wait to tell her how he was moved by her loyalty and obedience. He starts by saying:

> "O my love, you *are as* beautiful as Tirzah, lovely as Jerusalem, awesome as *an army* with banners!"
>
> (Song of Solomon 6:4)

Tirzah was one of the most attractive cities in the ancient world, which belonged to the Canaanites before it was conquered by Israel. It is considered the capital of the Gentiles; whose beauty is evident even among non-Jews. This allegory indicates that the devotion of the Bride can be perceived even by those who do not love God, or non-believers.

Solomon's temple was in the holy city of Jerusalem. It represents a place of worship and the habitation of God's presence. The bridegroom is saying, "You are like the holy city, where worship flows". The bride's obedience is a beautiful way of worshiping the bridegroom-king.

He also compares her to an army with banners. At that time, when an army won a battle, they captured the flags of those defeated. The king is saying, "You carry the evidence that you have won your internal battles". The most precious victories for God are those won on a personal level, in which we overcome the enemies of bitterness and unbelief.

The beloved is so undone by how the bride overcame that he says, "Turn your eyes away from me, for they have overcome me…" (Song of Solomon 6:5). His admiration for her is excessive, so much so that he cannot even look at her without being utterly moved. This is a deep revelation of how the heart of God is touched by our devotion to Him.

The Lord sees every one of our internal decisions. He is a God that is deeply involved in the human processes. He knows the price we pay and the right decisions we make when no one is looking. Psalm 56:8 says, "You number my wanderings; put my tears into Your bottle; *are they* not in Your book?". My prayer is that we will understand the Lord's narrative over our walk with him. It's easy to go through fiery trials and lose perspective on the fact that it actually produces lasting fruit. It is important to ask the Lord about how He sees us as well as His perspective on the various seasons of our relationship with Him.

The bridegroom begins to compliment the hair, teeth, and face of his beloved. These three aspects are the same ones mentioned when the bride's virtues were still flourishing. In this stage, she grows even more in devotion (hair), her ability to chew on the solid food of the Word (teeth), and her capacity to show godly emotions (face).

He also affirms, "There are sixty queens, And eighty concubines, And virgins without number. My dove, my perfect one, Is the only one…" (Song of Solomon 6:8-9). The queens, concubines, and virgins were components of the king's court, according to the hierarchy of that time. In this passage, they symbolize the heavenly hosts that are before the throne of God, seraphim, cherubs, archangels, and other beings.

Just as the bride is unique among the women of nobility, the Church is exclusively chosen to be the Bride of Christ, even among the other heavenly beings around the throne of God. The right to be made a suitable partner of the Resurrected Christ was not granted to angels, but to us, the Church of Jesus.

Then, the Holy Spirit asks the question, "Who is she who looks forth as the morning…" (Song of Solomon 6:10). The bride is being announced as the one who comes forth as the rising of the sun. She overcame the dark night of testing and is born again with the sun. She became so radiant and mature that she is unrecognizable.

The bride is described as fair as the moon, clear as the sun, and as awesome as an army with banners. The stars speak of the natural light that radiates from the bride. She is the Church of Christ who will be the salt and light throughout the whole world. Just as an army with banners will conquer the enemy and govern next to King Jesus.

All the trials she endured are turning her into a triumphant bride. She is being prepared to do the same works as the bridegroom. His partner's days of immaturity are behind her. In the next chapter, we will see how the partnership is consolidated.

9. Partnership in Maturity

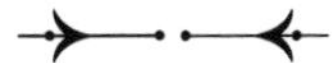

"I went down to the garden of nuts,

to see the verdure of the valley…

Return, return, O Shulamite;

Return, return, that we may look upon you!...

How beautiful are your feet in sandals, O prince's daughter!...

How fair and how pleasant you are, O love, with your delights!...

The wine goes *down* smoothly for my beloved…

I am my beloved's, and his desire is toward me…".

Song of Solomon 6:11-13, 7:1-10

Discipling Those that are Less Mature

This is a new season for the bride. She has been rooted in the soil of the Word and her fruits ignited a deep admiration in the King. After being anointed with the oil of obedience, doubly tested, and approved for mature love, she obtained a loyal heart free of offense.

In this next season, the bride has a desire to go to the gardens and observe the new shoots on the vines.

> "I went down to the garden of nuts, to see the verdure of the valley..."
>
> (Song of Solomon 6:11)

Even though she went through a long season consumed with herself and underwent personal processes, now is the time for the bride to go to the woods and see what is new on the plantations.

The new shoots that capture the bride's attention represent developing Christians. Just as she attended the maturation process, there is a new plantation of fresh shoots that also need to be cultivated into the fruits of Christian maturity. As mentioned in the beginning of the story, the king inspired her heart by announcing the coming harvest.

The isolated period of consolidating her virtues was necessary, but now the bride is ready and willing to participate in the growth of other Christians. She went through the same process and gained the knowledge and compassion necessary to contribute to the maturing of those who are a few seasons behind.

This speaks of Christian maturity that incites a desire to minister, mentor, and pastor people without the objective of power and fame, but to genuinely help and encourage others who are in the seasons that we have already overcome. The bride's enthusiasm when seeing new shoots bloom is due to the fact that she was treated with such patience and graciousness while she was maturing, and now she can do the same.

The key to leading people with a patient heart is to be moved by the same grace of God that was extended to us when we needed compassion and guidance. The divine lovingkindness that we received should be reciprocated to others when it is their turn to mature in the virtues of Christ. Our mission is to treat others the way the Lord treated us.

> "Before I was even aware, my soul had made me *as* the chariots of my noble people."
>
> (Song of Solomon 6:12)

The sudden feeling that her soul was like the people's chariots represents her newly acquired interest in people. She is surprised by this new love for the king's people. As a result of spending a great deal of time with the king, she is able to see his people as he does.

This is the work of the Holy Spirit leading us to have the same love that Christ has for people. When we get close to the heart of God, we get a perception of others through His eyes. Our values and desires are exchanged for His own. We begin to love what He loves, which is primarily people.

Paul the apostle demonstrated intense love and zeal for the church that he discipled. Many times, in his letters, he expressed a deep dedication to the growth of the Church.

> "So, affectionately longing for you, we were well pleased to impart to you not only the gospel of God, but also our own lives, because you had become dear to us."
>
> (1 Thessalonians 2:8)

The fulfillment of the first commandment, which is to love God above all things, leads us to carry out the second, which is to love our neighbor as ourselves (or how He loves us). The love that we receive from God guides us to the understanding of how much He loves our neighbor. This is the fruit of mature love becoming a fountain of wisdom for others.

I really believe in a leadership culture in which we do not lead because we are dominant figures or charismatic speakers, but because we have successfully walked out the maturity process that other Christians still need to experience. The problem with immature Christians assuming leadership roles is that they end up controlling others and abusing their position.

The result is that many people have traumatic experiences with religious leaders or with the church system, in general. Just like the fruit of maturity benefits many, the fruit of immaturity harms many. While this is unfortunate, we cannot simply dismiss the whole concept of gathering together as a Church.

"Extinguishing the Church is not God's intention, but rather purifying and sanctifying her to become the glorious Bride ready for His return."

I am a living testimony of how someone who hated the church system can become a person who fervently loves and intercedes for her. I hated the church format and thought we were going nowhere with those weekly meetings. My desire for God was sincere, but I was unconvinced that I could trust His people.

However, as I matured and let the Lord mold the desires of my heart to align with His own, I was naturally led to love the Church and believe in her. Extinguish the Church is not God's intention, but rather purifying and sanctifying her to become the glorious Bride ready for His return. It can be difficult to look at the Church today and imagine her as pure and holy, but the Bride will be that way in the last days.

The Two Responses from the Church

In reaction to the mature partnership of the bride, the daughters of Jerusalem say, "Return, return, O Shulamite; return, return, that we may look upon you!..." (Song of Solomon 6:13a). The daughters of Jerusalem respond to the bride with respect and admiration, asking her to come back so they can see her. This speaks of the sincere desire of immature Christians to learn from those who are more mature.

The next line comes from the watchmen. They say, "What would you see in the Shulamite — as it were, the dance of the two camps?" (Song of Solomon 6:13b). The watchmen are asking the daughters of Jerusalem why they want to see the bride. They ask, "What's so good about her?". This is the second reaction to the bride's maturity that Christians can have – jealousy and unbelief.

The dance of two camps speaks about the debate between Esau and Jacob in Genesis 32. This allegory refers to different reactions the characters in the story have toward the bride's fruit. Some of them react with joy and admiration (the daughters of Jerusalem), while others respond with sarcasm and jealousy (the watchman).

When we show the extraordinary fruit that comes from seasons lived out in obedience to God, people's reactions can vary. We are not always able to celebrate our victories, mainly when they are done in secret and no one sees the price we paid. People tend to look at the exterior without understanding the favor that people carry, believing they got it overnight.

However, despite the hostility and lack of understanding that may come, the Lord always has a way of justifying us. In this season, the daughters of Jerusalem represent Christians capable of discerning the virtues of the bride. Although immature, they are sincere and have real admiration for the bride. They are not discouraged by the unbelief of the watchmen and respond with sincerity.

The daughters of Jerusalem mention new characteristics of the bride's beauty. This shows how the Holy Spirit reveals the virtues to the Body of Christ, which should be learned and cultivated in Christian culture. As the virgins awoke, they were encouraged upon seeing the righteousness of the bride. They defend her by listing her attributes, "How beautiful are your feet in sandals, O prince's daughter!" (Song of Solomon 7:1). The feet of the bride speak of her announcing the good news of the gospel.

> "How beautiful upon the mountains, are the feet of him who brings good news..."
>
> (Isaiah 52:7)

The beloved is embracing the commission to make disciples and proclaim the good news of Christ.

They then describe the thighs and belly button of the bride. While the thighs speak of the capacity and strength to walk with God, the belly button signifies pregnancy. It is through the belly button that a child is nourished in the womb. This speaks of the perfect formation and nutrients the bride received when she underwent the maturing process with the Lord.

The belt refers to the abundance of the harvest. Song of Solomon 7:2 says, "...Your waist *is* a heap of wheat, Set about with lilies." The wheat is associated with prosperity and the lily means purity. The breasts of the bride are mentioned again. As before, they represent the ability to breastfeed those in need with the genuine milk of the Word (1 Peter 2:2).

The virgins go on to comment on the neck, eyes, and nose of the bride. The neck refers to the same characteristics as before, about remaining submissive. The eyes speak of the ability to receive understanding (Ephesians 1:18) and the nose symbolizes the capability to discern. The bride has the gifts of submissiveness, understanding, and discernment.

The bride's head represents the virtues of a renewed mind and a healthy thought life.

> "Your head *crowns* you like *Mount* Carmel, and the hair of your head *is* like purple…"
>
> (Song of Solomon 7:5)

> "For who has known the mind of the Lord that he may instruct Him? But we have the mind of Christ."
>
> (1 Corinthians 2:16)

The Groom's Three-fold Commission

After being defended by the virgins, the bride is vindicated by the Bridegroom. He celebrates her newfound maturity saying, "How fair and how pleasant you are, O love, with your delights! This stature of yours is like a palm tree…" (Song of Solomon 7:6-7). The bride grew, matured, and now her branches are bearing leaves. The evidence of her growth has produced pleasure and satisfaction in the beloved.

Song of Solomon 7:8 says, "I said, I will go up to the palm tree, I will take hold of its branches". When it says I will take hold of its branches, the bridegroom is promising to take the bride as his personal inheritance. Then, he admires three aspects which symbolize Jesus' three-fold commission to the Church.

Verse 8 continues by saying, "Let now your breasts be like clusters of the vine, The fragrance of your breath like apples". The breasts symbolize, once again, the ability of the beloved to nourish spiritual babies. It is the call to take care of immature Christians, and this is the first commission given to her. Paul says:

> "Let each of you look out not only for his own interests, but also for the interests of others."
>
> (Philippians 2:4)

Jesus also says:

> "For I was hungry and you gave Me food; I was thirsty and you gave Me drink; I was a stranger and you took Me in; I *was* naked and you clothed Me; inasmuch as you did *it* to one of the least of these My brethren, you did *it* to Me."
>
> (Matthew 25:35-40)

One of the commissions of Christian maturity is taking care of others. The second commission to the bride is that she releases the presence of the Holy Spirit.

> "The fragrance of your breath like apples."
>
> (Song of Solomon 7:8)

The breath speaks of the bride's inner life that reaches those around her. When we learn to walk in the power of the Holy Spirit, we are called to release His breath wherever we go.

The Word tells us in John 20:22 that Jesus breathed the Holy Spirit over His disciples, "And when He had said this, He breathed on *them,* and said, *Receive the Holy Spirit.*". In Acts 1:8 Jesus also declared, "But you shall receive power when the Holy Spirit has come upon you; and you shall be witnesses…".

The third and last commission to the bride / Church is to maintain intimacy with the bridegroom / Jesus. The passage says, "And the roof of your mouth [kisses] like the best wine…" (Song of Solomon 7:9). The kisses and the wine refer to the pleasure of intimacy between the bride and the bridegroom. Our mission is to continue maintaining intimate communion with Jesus, expressed through a life of prayer and love of the scriptures. This is the three-fold commission given from Jesus to the Church: take care of people, release the Holy Spirit, and maintain intimacy with Jesus.

> "God *is* faithful, by whom you were called into the fellowship of His Son, Jesus Christ our Lord."
>
> (1 Corinthians 1:9)

> "But you, when you pray, go into your room, and when you have shut your door, pray to your Father who *is* in the secret *place;* and your Father who sees in secret will reward you openly."
>
> (Matthew 6:6)

Mature Love Amid the Precarious

The phrase "I am my beloveds" is reoccurring and demonstrates the growing conviction of the bride that she whole-heartedly belongs to the bridegroom. Along the journey, the bride's sense of belonging to the Bridegroom grows. There is a conviction that nothing can separate her from his love (Romans 8:35-39).

> "Come, my beloved, let us go forth to the field; Let us lodge in the villages. There I will give you my love."
>
> (Song of Solomon 7:11-12)

The bride's suggestion is that they spend the night in the villages, that is, in the area where the peasants live, the poorest region of society. With this invitation, the bride is saying, "Let's go to the precarious places together! There you will see that my love is all Yours!".

> **"Our mission is to maintain our intimacy with Jesus, expressed in a life of prayer and a love of the scriptures."**

This speaks of a bride that is unafraid of going to areas in need or losing her intimacy with the bridegroom. When she says, "Let us see if the vine has budded, *whether* the grape blossoms are open…" (Song of Solomon 7:12), it shows faith that she will find beauty in the most hostile places, when she takes the bridegroom with her. This is how the Church will go to the farthest and neediest corners of the world to impart the gospel of Jesus.

As previously shared, Dwayne and I served for many years as missionaries in the field. At that time, we did missions in places like the Soviet Russia and India. Despite the extreme spiritual coldness and deprivation of these places, amazing things happened when we were there proclaiming the name of Jesus. In the midst of the danger, we witnessed extraordinary fruit.

The mature bride believed that she would find remarkable fruit, even in the most distant and hostile lands. She is willing to go to the ends of the earth and "give her love", which is a testament of her dedication to lead others to Jesus. When we are immature, we do not know how to operate in uncomfortable and unstable conditions.

Once the bride bore the fruit of maturity and found pleasure in touching the bridegroom with her obedience, she was willing to go to dangerous and inconvenient places. Her sense of stability is not in her circumstances, but in the mature confidence that has been developed in her beloved. This is the sacrificial expression of the love of God flowing through us to the world.

173 The last verse in chapter 7 of Song of Solomon says, "…and at our gates are pleasant *fruits,* all manner, new and old, which I have laid up for you, my beloved" (Song of Solomon 7:13). In her mature partnership with the bridegroom, the beloved is saying, "Enjoy the fruits of our labors". The harvest is just beginning, and the fruits will be eternal.

10. Contemplanting the Journey

"Oh, that you were like my brother,

who nursed at my mother's breasts!...

Who *is* this coming up from the wilderness,

Leaning upon her beloved?... Set me as a seal upon your heart,

as a seal upon your arm; for love *is* as strong as death…

What shall we do for our sister, In the day when she is spoken for?...

My own vineyard is before me…

Makc haste, my beloved, and be like a gazelle, or a young stag,

On the mountains of spices."

Song of Solomon 8:1-14

The Bride Leaning on the Bridegroom

The last chapter in Song of Solomon begins with an exclamation, "Oh, that you were like my brother… *If* I should find you outside, I would kiss you; I would not be despised" (Song of Solomon 8:1). In the time that this song was written, a woman could not show physical affection for a non-relative in public. So, an engaged woman would not be able to show affection for her fiancé in public, but she could for her brother. Hence, the bride is almost yelling, "I want everyone to know how much I love you!". In addition to that statement, she wants people to understand the twofold understanding that Jesus is fully God and fully man. The Bible tells us that Jesus was not received as the Son of God since most saw him as just a man. They say, "Is this not the carpenter's son?" (Matthew 13:55). The bride expresses her desire to see Him recognized as God, even though she does not understand the mystery of His concurrent humanity and divinity. Colossians 2:9 says, "For in Him dwells all the fullness of the Godhead bodily".

In the face of this difficulty, the bride decides to position her heart to depend totally on God. She says, "His left hand *is* under my head, and his right hand embraces me" (Song of Solomon 8:3). Remember that the left hand represents the invisible sovereign acts of God, while the right hand signifies those that are visible. She is counting on divine intervention to complete His work in her as well as in those who do not believe yet.

The passage then says, "Who *is* this coming up from the wilderness, leaning upon her beloved?" (Song of Solomon 8:5). For the third time, the Holy Spirit is the one who asks the questions and announces the characters. The question is asked with wonder and amazement, "Who is the lovely bride that we now see, coming out of the wilderness of testing and leaning on her beloved?"

This speaks of the bride's incredible transformation. Previously, she was immature with virtues not yet formed. Nevertheless, once she submitted herself to the divine processes, she became resistant to adverse circumstances, rooted in the knowledge of the bridegroom's virtues (knowledge of Christ), finally demonstrating mature love and willingness to sacrifice.

When it says, "coming out of the wilderness", the Holy Spirit points out that she overcame the wilderness seasons of her life. All of us have endured the wilderness and testing. Even Jesus was taken into the wilderness and tested by the Holy Spirit (Matthew 4:1). That happened so that He would be ready to say, "Not my will but yours be done" in Gethsemane, making the decision to obey even unto death on the cross (Luke 22:42).

The Holy Spirit is the one who forges the ability to love God above all things, resulting in total obedience. He said, "Greater love has no one than this, than to lay down one's life for his friends" (John 15:14). Our demonstration of obedience is our test of love, as in "He who has My commandments and keeps them, it is he who loves Me…" (John 14:21).

The passage describes the bride as "leaning on her beloved", as she is completely reliant on her bridegroom. This is the image of the Church learning to put all her trust in Christ. As an illustration of when we embrace the processes of perfecting our Christian character, we become totally dependent on God.

The Word says, "Trust in the Lord with all your heart, and lean not on your own understanding" (Proverbs 3:5). The commandment of the Lord to the Church is to trust Him with all of our heart, not relying on our own methods, reasons, and strength. This is the only way that we can victoriously walk out of the wilderness seasons.

In fact, the whole earthly experience for those who are born again in God, is compared to the wilderness. We are strangers on the Earth with a life journey that is not free from opposition and discomfort until Jesus returns with complete restoration. Only then will there be no more pain and adversities to overcome.

Jesus said, "...In the world you will have tribulation; but be of good cheer, I have overcome the world" (John 16:33). He again taught us by saying, "For our citizenship is in heaven, from which we also eagerly wait for the Savior, the Lord Jesus Christ" (Philippians 3:20). The wait for the Bridegroom and the desire for Him to restore all things, until there is no more pain on the Earth, is the fruit of a mature Christian walk.

The success of the journey comes from learning to completely depend on the Lord, coming out of the desert "leaning" on Him. It is He who sustains and strengthens us in the good and bad moments of our lives. However, this does not concern our ability to use strengths and talents to reach success, but our capacity to trust God and leave the final result to Him.

Maybe the Lord removes our "crutches" along the journey, putting us in a position of learning to rest in Him. He wants to show us that it is not beauty, money, power, or talent that will guarantee eternal fruits. The mature bride has a heart totally leaning on her beloved, not material or fleeting things. What's more, He is the One who leads us through the wilderness triumphantly.

The Seal of Mature Love

The bridegroom now remembers the period when he comforted his beloved under the apple tree. It is as if he is saying, "Remember the time that I refreshed you under the scolding sun". When we remember how the Lord guided us in past seasons, we become more confident that He will continue to strengthen us. He is our guarantee that we will end the journey well.

The passage then says, "There your mother brought you forth; there she *who* bore you brought *you* forth" (Song of

Solomon 8:5). That is, with "labor pains", a mature bride was conceived. Paul uses this same symbolism in Galatians 4:19, "My little children, for whom I labor in birth again until Christ is formed in you". Christ is formed in His bride through labor pains or adversity.

> **"The mature bride has a heart totally leaning on her beloved, not material or fleeting things."**

In Song of Solomon 8:6, the bridegroom says, "Set me as a seal upon your heart, As a seal upon your arm". Some theologians say that this phrase comes from the bride. I tend to agree with those that believe that the seal refers to a mark on the bride's heart and arm. It is she that needs to be sealed, not him. 2 Corinthians 1:22 says of the Lord, "Who also has sealed us and given us the Spirit in our hearts as a guarantee".

In the time that Song of Solomon was written, the king's official documents were sealed with the royal seal and sent with an armed escort. If the document ended up in the wrong hands, the messenger could be considered a traitor and even killed. For this reason, it is a strong declaration. He is saying, "Ask Me to bestow an exclusive and non-transferable love".

The Beloved wants our love to be completely surrendered and devoted. He wants us to have eyes for only Him, saving us from any other lover or idol. A bride sealed with divine love means one who is committed, never returning to her past loves, such as the distractions, comforts, and privileges of this age. A bride who has an undivided heart.

When we cry out to the Lord to put His seal of love on us, He takes pleasure in keeping us from failing. This turns our fragile willful cry into activated divine help, never ceasing to remain in Him.

My friend Mike Bickle, author of many books and the director of IHOP, who has tirelessly preached on the Bridal Paradigm, told me that in July 1988, God spoke to him about this passage. While reading it, he began to pray, "Jesus seal my heart with Your fiery love". In that very moment, the prophet Bob Jones called him from across the country to say that the Lord audibly said that He was releasing grace to the Body of Christ to walk out the reality of Song of Solomon 8:6-7. This speaks of the message of the first commandment lived out by the Church throughout the whole Earth. The Lord also instructed Bob to tell Mike to concentrate on preaching this message. And this is what he has been doing ever since.

The scripture says, "For love *is as* strong as death, Jealousy *as* cruel as the grave" (Song of Solomon 8:6). Love that is "as cruel as the grave" means that it is as far-reaching and demanding as death. This is where we see the expression of God's jealous love. Since the Old Testament, the Lord exhorts His people to not have other gods. He said to Israel several times, "You shall have no other gods before Me" (Deuteronomy 5:7).

The Lord is jealous and will not share His bride with other idols. Therefore, He uses the allegory of marriage to represent His covenant with His church – an exclusive love that cannot be shared with other lovers. Exodus 34:14 says, "For you shall worship no other god, for the Lord, whose name *is* Jealous, *is* a jealous God".

Generally, we think that the carved images made from metal and dirt are the only ones that displease God. However, in this day and age, we idolize things like comfort, reputation, pleasures, money, prestige, people, among others. Anything that means more to us than the Lord is an idol in our lives.

But He guarantees, "...your embers are embers of fire, with vehement flames", that is, the Lord is committed to consuming our competing passions with the embers of His holy fire. The fiery passion for Christ in our hearts will be stronger than earthly desires. The Lord will send an all-consuming fire to devour all hindrances that get in the way of loving Him absolutely.

> **"A bride sealed with divine love means one who is committed, never returning to her past loves, such as the distractions, comforts and privileges of this age."**

Thus, we can ask the Lord to seal us with His jealous love, keeping us vigilant so that our devotion is never diminished. Until Christ's return, it is He who will preserve us. Paul says, "who will also confirm you to the end, *that you may be* blameless in the day of our Lord Jesus Christ" (1 Corinthians 1:8).

The passage continues, "Many waters cannot quench love, nor can the floods drown it..." (Song of Solomon 8:7). Again, this is an analogy that love can withstand instability. Even if a tsunami comes our way, we will stand firm. This is the love that is described in Romans 8:38-39, where death, nor life can separate us.

Water that puts out fire, refers to our supernatural help from the Holy Spirit to maintain our love for God. How can fire not be quenched by many waters? It can only be something divine. The most difficult of life's circumstances is when we see the supernatural help of God sustaining our love for Him.

The next affirmation reveals the nature of the love of God, "If a man would give for love all the wealth of his house, it would be utterly despised…" (Song of Solomon 8:7). This means that we cannot put monetary value on the love given to us. God's love for us is extravagant and undeserved; it cannot be earned through good deeds or sacrificial measures.

Even if we gave everything in exchange for this love, we would still be unworthy of the price Jesus paid. However, even when we seek to repay Him with our sacrifices of love, the merit is still God's. We are only able to love because the Lord first loved us (1 John 4:19). This love does not begin with us, but rather Him, so we should never seek special recognition for the extravagant commitments we make.

Love's reward is to love and be loved, the reason we were created. God did not call us into existence out of boredom or domination. Quite the opposite, He freely showers us with His loving nature. We were inserted into the love of the Trinity, because the Father loves the Son, who loves the Holy Spirit. John 15:9 says, "As the Father loved Me, I also have loved you; abide in My love".

Jesus told us to abide in the love we received from the Father. After learning what love is through His example, we should simply remain willing to give and demonstrate what He first granted us. For this reason, the Lord is the only One who can sustain us in love, not our own strength.

The guarantee that we are loved does not come from us. The Lord Himself ensures that our covenant with God is unbroken. Even though our contribution is submission to the processes as well as obedience, the love of God for us is always the strongest element that guarantees this eternal relationship. Our human love is fragmented, but in Him we learn and experience an unbreakable and supernatural love.

The Bride's Intercession

The next passage is often underestimated by scholars due to misinterpretation. However, we observe this text as an important representation of the mature bride's intercession for the immature bride. It says, "We have a little sister, and she has no breasts. What shall we do for our sister, In the day when she is spoken for?" (Song of Solomon 8:8).

This question can be paraphrased as "What can we do for the immature bride when she is expected to be mature enough to marry?". This speaks of the Bride's burden for the maturation of the entire Body of Christ in love before Jesus returns for the marriage of the Lamb (Revelation 19:7).

The bride says, "If she *is* a wall, we will build upon her, a battlement of silver; and if she *is* a door, we will enclose her with boards of cedar" (Song of Solomon 8:9). This signifies that the Church will be edified until she becomes a mature bride. Her structure will be a work in progress until she is ready as with silver and cedar.

The bride then declares, "I *am* a wall, and my breasts like towers; then I became in his eyes, as one who found peace" (Song of Solomon 8:10). Demonstrating that she now possesses a sense of identity, she is able to declare how God sees her. The wall speaks of an altruistic motivation, the towers refer to the ability to edify. To be "one who found peace" denotes that the bride overcame by removing emotional obstacles.

It is the mature part of the Church that prays and intercedes so that those who are immature can grow. As the Bridegroom saw the virtues of the Bride when they were still invisible, she now believes that her "younger sister" will also reach maturity by the end of the story. Likewise, although we may look at the Church today and notice its many flaws, the mature Bride still believes in the potential of the immature Bride and intercedes for her.

The intercession of the Church is a key piece for the glorious Bride to be edified. In fact, the persistent intercession of the Bride is what will hasten the return of Jesus, as He will come in response to the cry of the saints.

> "And shall God not avenge His own elect who cry out day and night to Him, though He bears long with them? I tell you that He will avenge them speedily. Nevertheless, when the Son of Man comes, will He really find faith on the earth?"
>
> (Luke 18:7-9)

A cry for justice will be established on the Earth before Jesus returns, which is in response to the Church's unceasing worship and intercession for His return. Only a vigilant Church will be able to endure the events of the end times.

> "Watch therefore, and pray always that you may be counted worthy to escape all these things that will come to pass, and to stand before the Son of Man."
>
> (Luke 21:36)

> "But the day of the Lord will come as a thief in the night, in which the heavens will pass away with a great noise... Therefore, since all these things will be dissolved, what manner *of persons* ought you to be in holy conduct and godliness, looking for and hastening the coming of the day of God..."
>
> (2 Peter 3:10-12)

The apostle Peter believes that by living in a godly manner, we are hastening the coming of the Lord. It is for this reason that the theme of Christian maturity has become imperative today, since the formation of a glorious Church is evidence of Christ's imminent return. The Word says that in the end times, the Church will be resilient enough to withstand unprecedented persecution.

The opposition against the Church will become even more intense, as it is already manifesting. Secular agendas and principles are strongly infiltrating the media, education systems, culture, and government. While darkness is gaining ground, it is essential that the light of the Church expands its territory as well, overpowering iniquity.

The Church in the last days will sustain its faith and love for God while living in a worldly system. As it is a Church that does not negotiate its principles nor make concessions to darkness, remaining loyal to God in an era of false idols. Forged in mature love, the Bride is committed to confessing Jesus as Lord to the point of losing her life if necessary.

Chances are, we have not experienced a level of physical persecution in the western countries that we live in today. We are not being executed in squares or tortured to death, however, this happens in other countries. People are giving their lives for loving Christ, where systems, governments, and other religions are intolerant to the Christian faith.

All twelve apostles in the New Testament, except John, were martyred because of the gospel. In the context of the end times, Jesus warned His disciples, "But before all these things, they will lay their hands on you and persecute *you,* delivering *you* up to the synagogues and prisons. You will be brought before kings and rulers for My name's sake" (Luke 21:12).

> **"In the last days, the systems in power will become more and more intolerant to the Christian faith. However, as the darkness grows so shall the light. I believe the small trials that we have overcome prepare us to be unshakable in the great trial at the end of the age."**

Does this mean that all of us will be martyrs? No. Is martyrdom the only way to show that we learned how to love God above all things? Also no. But we need to take into consideration that in the last days, the systems in power will become more and more intolerant to the Christian faith. However, as the darkness grows so shall the light. I believe the small trials that we have overcome prepare us to be unshakable in the great trial at the end of the age. Our motivation to endure will be the comfort of knowing that

Christ's return is forthcoming. Consequently, our hearts will burn with desire for His return.

> "Therefore, be patient, brethren, until the coming of the Lord. See *how* the farmer waits for the precious fruit of the earth, waiting patiently for it until it receives the early and latter rain. You also be patient. Establish your hearts, for the coming of the Lord is at hand."
>
> (James 5:7-8)

Jesus' Last Commission to the Bride

In this last stretch, the symbolism of the Song of Solomon points to a promise of eternal reward. The bride mentions that Solomon's vineyard was lent to the keepers. They were to return a thousand pieces of silver to the king. This illustration reminds me of the parable in Matthew 25, where the servants received the valuable talents from their master and had to multiply their investments or live wisely. The multiplication of talents represents the burden of mankind to be accountable to the Lord for what He has given us. One day, we will stand before the Lord and rewarded according to our acts.

> "For the Son of Man will come in the glory of His Father with His angels, and then He will reward each according to his works."
>
> (Matthew 16:27)

> "And behold, I am coming quickly, and My reward *is* with Me, to give to everyone according to his work."
>
> (Revelation 22:12)

The mature Bride recognizes her responsibility to present her personal works on the day of the Lord.

> "My vineyard, my very own, is before me; you, O Solomon, may have the thousand, and the keepers of the fruit two hundred."
>
> (Song of Solomon 8:12)

With these words, the Bride is saying, "I am responsible for my life, because I know that each one will be held accountable on the day of the Lord". The day that we are face to face with the just Judge, we cannot blame other people for those acts presented. Each one will stand alone before the Lord to take responsibility for what is theirs alone.

Even though I have spent many years at Dwayne's side, sharing most decisions and actions with him, I will still stand alone before the Lord in eternity. I will be judged for every decision and personal attitude, unable to ask Dwayne to speak up and be my personal reference. I will stand alone before the Lord to give an individual, non-transferable account. Remembering that perfect love casts out fear (1 John 4:18). I do not fear standing before the Lord. Nonetheless, I do live intentionally as it is a sobering appointment up ahead. The way in which I love God and others matters. Knowing that day is coming gives me perspective on ensuring that I weed the "garden of my heart", eliminating offense until then (Philippians 2;9-11).

> "Now if anyone builds on this foundation *with* gold, silver, precious stones, wood, hay, straw, each one's work will become clear; for the Day will declare it, because it will be revealed by fire;

> and the fire will test each one's work, of what sort it is. If anyone's work which he has built on *it* endures, he will receive a reward."
>
> (1 Corinthians 3:12-14)

Going back to the context of Song of Solomon 8, the bridegroom king explains in verse 13, "O you who dwell in the gardens, with companions listening for your voice; let me hear it". The Bridegroom asks to hear the bride's voice (prayer) and that others would hear it (proclamation). This request represents the last commission that the Bridegroom gives her, that she would be a relevant Church. Being a voice means actively waiting on and listening to the Lord while reaching others. The Church of Christ is called to be relevant and influence the world throughout.

> "That you may become blameless and harmless, children of God without fault in the midst of a crooked and perverse generation, among whom you shine as lights in the world."
>
> (Philippians 2:15)

The glorious Church is promised a place of impact. Jesus said:

> "You are the light of the world. A city that is set on a hill cannot be hidden. Nor do they light a lamp and put it under a basket, but on a lampstand, and it gives light to all *who are* in the house."
>
> (Matthew 5:14-15)

Finally, the bride makes the request that ends her entire trajectory in the book of Song of Solomon. After receiving the call to become a relevant Church, she says, "Make haste, my beloved, and be like a gazelle or a young stag on the mountains of spices" (Song of Solomon 8:14).

The ultimate desire of the bride is that the bridegroom returns urgently to her. This request is resembles the one described in the final verses of the Bible, found in Revelation 22:17, which says, "And the Spirit and the bride say, *come!* And let him who hears say, *come!* And let him who thirst come. Whoever desires, let him take the water of life freely". At the end of the story, she cries out along with the Holy Spirit: "Maranatha!". This is the last prayer that the Bride records in the scriptures, now a suitable partner who has learned to yearn for Christ's return.

There is not a better way to end this story. The Bride was accepted in her immaturity, comforted in her adversity, and disciplined in her self-indulgence. Her virtues were affirmed, tested in two ways, and finally approved to be the Bride of Christ. In the end, it is her duty to be a watchful and intercessory Bride, looking forward to the King's return and their wedding day.

Like Paul, who successfully ended his earthly journey, we should rejoice in the reward coming to those who love the Lord's return. As in:

> "I have fought the good fight, I have finished the race, I have kept the faith. Finally, there is laid up for me the crown of righteousness, which the Lord, the righteous Judge, will give to me on that Day, and not to me only but also to all who have loved His appearing."
>
> (2 Timothy 4:7-8)

The crown is reserved for those who walk out the journey of producing mature and lasting love to the very end. They are those that yearn for the moment when the distance no longer exists, and their hunger is finally satisfied as a result of His return. The King will be so much more than what we learned from the scriptures or what we felt through the Holy Spirit, as we see His glorious face at long last. This marvelous day will make each and every step of our journey worth it all.

Final Prayer

My prayer for you is that you can see the Lord helping you throughout your journey, filling you with courage to walk in all seasons of your life. May you realize Jesus' pleasure over you as you move toward spiritual maturity, knowing that He was present throughout the process, fulfilling His purposes in your life. I pray that the first commandment will become your priority and that understanding Jesus as the Bridegroom will strengthen you and produce spiritual depth while you wait for His return.

Jennifer Roberts

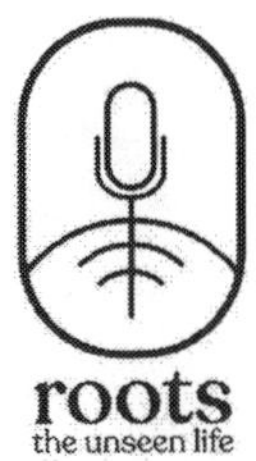

Roots the Unseen Life podcast helps give followers of Jesus the tools and the wisdom they need to walk out their Christian faith in a turbulent society. Dwayne and Jennifer Roberts give practical guidance to help navigate our ever-shifting culture. With their combined life and ministry experience they guide people in overcoming difficulty and failure and navigating success while teaching deep biblical truths.

Watch it on their YouTube channel, Dwayne and Jennifer, or listen to it on all digital platforms!

Dwayne & Jennifer

Check out Dwayne and Jennifer's website for tools and resources to help you walk out your faith. They give helpful and practical wisdom on navigating the highs and lows of life. They have blogs, podcast episodes, masterclasses, and other resources and exclusive content to help you along your journey.

DwayneandJennifer.com

Masterclasses

Join Dwayne and Jennifer as they take you on guided journeys through different topics and books of the bible in their masterclasses. This masterclasses are a series of short yet rich videos that are meant to teach you about God, your relationship with Him, and how to walk out your faith.

Check them out at DwayneandJennifer.com

Made in the USA
Monee, IL
24 April 2022